Dying
for a
Drink

Dying for a Drink

What You Should Know About Alcoholism

ANDERSON SPICKARD, M.D.
AND
BARBARA R. THOMPSON

WORD BOOKS
PUBLISHER
WACO, TEXAS

A DIVISION OF
WORD, INCORPORATED

Library of Congress Cataloging in Publication Data

Spickard, Anderson, 1931–
    Dying for a drink.

    Includes index.
    1. Alcoholism. 2. Alcoholism—Treatment. I. Thompson,
Barbara R. II. Title. [DNLM: 1. Alcohol Drinking—
popular works. 2. Alcoholism—popular works.
WM 274 S754d]
RC565.S67 1985   616.86'1   85-3343
ISBN 0-8499-0467-6

We are indebted to numerous friends and family members for their concern and support during the writing of this book. We particularly want to thank our editor, Kathleen Mohr, for her outstanding work; as well as Linda Jensen, Connie Nash, and Dan Raines for their invaluable contributions.

A Note to Readers

Any use of masculine pronouns in this book is not intended to be discriminating. We have attempted to address equally the problems of alcoholism from the perspective of both males and females. However, to use both "he" and "she" in every appropriate instance seemed confusing and cumbersome. So, for clarity and consistency, we have used throughout the book masculine pronouns, except in those cases where the gender of the antecedent is clearly identifiable.

The stories and case histories in this book are based on interviews and real experiences. However, names and sometimes other minor details have been changed to protect the privacy of individuals.

Contents

Foreword

In this decade, the front line in the battle against disease is in the area of alcoholism and other chemical dependencies. Until recently the people of our country had only begun to address this major public health problem which has now grown to epidemic proportions and is attacking the very moral fiber of our country. I believe it is time for the church, the medical profession, and the academic communities of America to understand this disease and mobilize their resources to be a part of the solution to this national problem.

This book, *Dying for a Drink,* is written by two people whose backgrounds in medicine, the church, and working with the problems of addiction enable them to present their message in a way that can be related to and understood by members of the Christian community. It is obviously the result of years of firsthand experience in treating this tragic disease which is one of the most disruptive forces to the family structure.

Approaching the problem from the viewpoint of each family member—husband, wife, children, and parents—*Dying for a Drink* reaches out and grabs you with an examination of the destructive evil power that works through addiction. It explains the cunning and baffling power of denial that grips not only the sick person and family, but also the health professionals and church leaders who are not trained in understanding what is happening.

The authors have a message that is desperately needed in every church in America. It should be read with an open mind and an open heart, because through these

11

pages comes the positive power of training, education, experience, prayer, and faith! You may not agree with all you read here, but I can testify by my personal experience that this message is one of healing on a front line of spiritual warfare—where no one can travel without an absolute faith that God is the force behind these recovery processes.

This book should be read by every person concerned with alcoholism or chemical dependency and placed on a shelf in the library of every concerned church in America. My hope is that the message herein will become an instrument to mobilize the church to meet the needs of those who are affected by these deadly diseases.

Harold E. Hughes
U.S. Senate, retired

Introduction

Tom Jordan was an alcoholic. He was a carpenter in a small town, and every night his neighbors saw his pickup truck parked in front of the local bar. A few minutes after midnight, he would weave his way down the road and stumble up the front steps of his house. His wife, looking tired and worn, always waited up for him and helped him to bed.

One night, for reasons no one ever knew, Tom went with his next-door neighbor to a revival meeting at the town church. He smelled of alcohol, but he listened carefully to the Gospel message. At the end of the service, when an invitation to repentance was given, Tom went to the altar. With tears streaming down his cheeks, he gave his life to Jesus and promised never to drink again.

Tom was sober for nine months. Then he slipped. He went on a three-week drinking binge, but when it was over, he came back to the church. He asked the congregation to forgive him, and vowed that he had taken his last drink. The church members were impressed by his sincerity and humility. They encouraged Tom to be more faithful in daily Bible study and not to neglect Wednesday-night prayer meeting.

Tom attended church at every opportunity and memorized long passages of Scripture. For six months he remained sober. Then he fell "off the wagon" and went on a drinking binge that lasted over three months. When he finally sobered up, he returned to church. His fellow believers laid hands on him and asked God to deliver him from drink. The church elders spoke to him sternly, charging him to make up his mind never to drink again and to pray, believing that God would help him. Tom attended healing services and claimed victory over drinking.

Despite these efforts, Tom began to drink again. He continued the cycle of drinking and sobering up for several years, until he was once again a daily drinker. He still attended church, but he always came late and sat in the back row, looking at his shoes. When members of the congregation shook his hand, he smiled gratefully, but in his eyes there was a pained expression of defeat.

It wasn't long before some members of the congregation wanted to ask Tom to leave. His heart was hard, they said, and his presence was an embarrassment—almost an insult. Furthermore, they claimed, for weaker Christians Tom's chronic drinking created vague, unspoken anxieties about God's power to rescue human beings from sin. Other church members disagreed. Tom had a problem with alcohol, but he was still a good man. There was hope for him. Some day, after enough prayer and good preaching, he would give up drinking. It was just a matter of time—and patience.

After nine years of attending church, Tom finally decided that he had taken his last drink. "There's only one way people like me stop drinking," he told a friend early one evening. "That's by going to heaven. I don't think I can wait any longer." Tom went home and took a vacuum cleaner hose out of the closet. He hooked the hose to the exhaust pipe of his pickup truck, ran it into the truck, and rolled up the windows. Then he climbed in the front seat and started the engine. When his wife found him in the morning, he was dead.

Every year thousands of alcoholics like Tom Jordan pass through the church looking for a way to stop drinking. Some of them find it. The vast majority, however, become victims of "the myth of the quick fix." They are persuaded by well-meaning Christian believers that if only they say the right words, pray the right prayers, or find the right person to lay hands on them, their addiction will miraculously disappear.

It's true that some people are instantly healed of addiction. Sometime ago, one of my alcoholic patients, a paraplegic, came to my office and announced, "Doc, I've been saved, and I've had my last drink." His craving for alcohol disappeared immediately and, as far as I know, it never returned.

Yet for every alcoholic like this patient, there are thousands who seek help from the church and walk away from the altar with their anguish deepened and their faith shattered. A few choose to continue attending services, hoping one day to find the secret key to sobriety. Many of these, like Tom Jordan, are "healed" of their addiction time and time again. They drink, repent, sober up—sometimes for as long as two years or more—and then get drunk again. Their failure to stop drinking is often attributed to a spiritual weakness or a mysterious inability to appropriate God's grace.

It is a strangely well-kept secret that the vast majority of alcoholics who stop drinking, both inside and outside the church, do so because they employ time-tested tools and principles for staying sober. Alcoholism is a problem of "the whole person," and recovery from its comprehensive damage takes hard work, retraining—and time. While occasionally an alcoholic is miraculously delivered from his *physical* craving for alcohol, there is no instant cure for the *spiritual* and *psychological* damage inflicted by chemical addiction.*

The bad news is that it is difficult to overcome addiction. The good news is that today over one million men, women, and teenagers are sober because, by the grace of God, they are following a rigorous spiritual program of recovery. This program is a comprehensive approach to addiction which neither denies the power of the Holy

---

*While the contents of this book focus on alcohol addiction, the similarities between alcohol and other drug addictions are greater than the differences. The differences are primarily in physical effects, diagnostic tests, and medical management of withdrawal. The means of treatment, as well as the spiritual principles involved, are currently the same for all addictive substances.

Spirit nor overlooks the alcoholic's ultimate responsibility for his own ongoing recovery. All over the world, alcoholics whose lives have been devastated by their drinking are being healed in their bodies, minds, emotions, spirits, and relationships. Equally as important, the families of alcoholics—parents, wives, husbands, children—are confronting their own damaged lives and finding healing for their deepest wounds.

To participate in the joyful process of recovery from addiction, we must ask ourselves hard questions and be prepared to change long-standing opinions. Why do people become alcoholics? Is addiction a sin? Is it a disease? Why can't alcoholics see their problem and help themselves? Why do family members frequently become as sick as the alcoholic? What about the role of Alcoholics Anonymous, treatment centers, and healing services? On what basis should we make decisions about our personal drinking habits?

In my twenty years of medical practice, few experiences have had a resurrection quality equal to that of watching alcoholics and their families leave behind the living death of addiction. Today, while much of the world staggers under the weight of chemical addiction, the church is called upon to be a vessel of this resurrection power. It is my hope that Christian believers will take the lead in serving this suffering generation with practical and realistic efforts.

God's grace has invaded the lives of thousands of alcoholics. I trust that this book will be a means of his grace in your lives as well.

Anderson Spickard, Jr., M.D.

1

A Spreading Epidemic

One out of every ten drinkers—up to ten million Americans. . . . We find them at cocktail parties or at church, in an executive office suite or behind the door of our own homes. In increasing numbers, they attend our local high school. They are middle-class, rich, and poor; white, black, Spanish, and Indian. Some are melancholy, some euphoric; some are angry, others docile. They worship in synagogues, cathedrals, large evangelical churches, and small charismatic prayer meetings.

These men, women, and children have one thing in common. *They are alcoholics.* The intoxicating liquid which over a hundred million Americans drink for pleasure, they drink from necessity. Slowly but certainly, if left unchecked, they drink themselves to death, insanity, or institutionalization.

Only 5 percent of addicted drinkers live on skid row; the rest are our neighbors. Some are infants born with the smell of alcohol on their breath: alcoholic mothers are the number three cause of birth defects associated with mental retardation. Some are grammar school children: in Nebraska, boys and girls as young as eight years old are suffering from cirrhosis, delirium tremens (DTs), and other alcohol-related problems.[1] Others are among the 3.3 million teenagers all over the United States who bounce back and forth between alcohol and illegal drugs. And a growing number are housewives, "hidden alcoholics"

17

who secretly sip their lives away and baffle unsuspecting
husbands with erratic, unpredictable behavior.

On the far end of the spectrum are the elderly. Loneliness, a sense of uselessness, and doctors who prescribe
"one drink at bedtime" are sending senior citizens into
alcoholism at record rates. Isolation and the respectability of alcohol make it easy for the aged to hide the
amount of their consumption and the rapid progression of
their addiction. More than one grandmother has taken
her first drink at the age of sixty, only to be admitted
within a few years to a hospital detoxification ward by a
shocked and disbelieving family.

Sadly, neither doctors, mental health professionals, nor
church members are equipped to handle this growing epidemic of addiction. The average doctor prescribes tranquilizers for his bothersome alcoholic patients; the alcoholic loves a Valium with his drink. Psychiatrists and
psychologists go to great lengths to uncover childhood
traumas and Freudian alibis; alcoholics gratefully accept
any explanation that justifies their need for a bottle. Finally, the typical well-intentioned Christian, of whom I
was one, hits the alcoholic over the head with his Bible.
The alcoholic, with his head aching and his heart in anguish, takes another drink.

Amidst this overwhelming ineffectiveness, the good
news is that there is hope for alcoholics. The pronounced
sense of helplessness with which our society approaches
addiction is completely misleading. This pessimism in part
accounts for why 90 percent of all alcoholics never enter
treatment programs, but it overlooks the remarkable percentage of addicted drinkers who, *having received appropriate help,* are living sober, productive lives.

Our own journey from helplessness to effective action
begins with an investigation into the causes of addiction.
Why do people become alcoholics? Recent medical research provides some startling answers to this question
and brings us face to face with a sobering fact. Few of us,
if any, can say, "It could never happen to me."

2

It Could Never Happen to Me

Betty Wilson married a good man. Bill was a successful contractor, a kind husband and father, and he never forgot a birthday or an anniversary. He coached Little League teams, led Boy Scout troops, and attended the First Baptist Church every Sunday. On Wednesday morning he went to prayer meeting, and on Saturday morning he ate breakfast with the Christian Businessmen's Fellowship. None of these gatherings, for Bill, was merely a religious ritual; he was a devout Christian sincerely desiring to practice his faith.

Bill's stumbling block was alcohol. He drank steadily throughout the early years of his marriage and, by his mid-forties, was a full-blown alcoholic. This condition caused both Bill and Betty enormous anguish. Every morning, in their private devotions, they begged God to take away Bill's desire to drink. Every evening, by six o'clock, Bill was drunk.

When Bill and Betty first visited my office in 1978, Bill was drinking a fifth of vodka a day. His history and a physical exam confirmed that he was in the late stages of alcoholism and unlikely to recover without professional help. I strongly urged Bill to attend a local treatment center, and I directed Betty to a grassroots organization for the family and friends of alcoholics.

Betty, whose own father was an alcoholic, went to meetings and began reading the latest literature available on alcoholism. Bill consulted with his children and his minister, and he discovered that they were just as skeptical about professional treatment as he was. He decided not to follow my advice and once more determined to stop drinking by his own will power.

Two years later, during a heavy drinking episode, Bill had a heart attack. While lying on his hospital bed, he realized that he was powerless over alcohol and that he needed help to stop drinking. He agreed to enter a treatment center as soon as he was physically able, and he began educating himself about addiction.

One week after Bill's discharge from the hospital, Betty phoned to say that he was lying collapsed on the kitchen floor. When I arrived a few minutes later, Bill was dead.

After Bill's death, Betty lived alone. Within a year her home was burglarized, and the possessions which she and Bill had gathered together disappeared. Betty plunged into a deep depression, and it was only with considerable effort that she forced herself out of bed each morning.

One evening, on her way home from work, Betty stopped by the store for a bottle of pink champagne. She had one drink, and the tightness in her chest disappeared. For the first time in months, she slept soundly and woke up feeling relaxed and refreshed.

Within six weeks, Betty was drinking two glasses of champagne a night. During the workday, she hid her sadness from her co-workers behind a mask of indifference; at night, she rushed home to dissolve her grief in alcohol. "That bottle should have been labeled, 'Take as needed for pain,'" remembers Betty. "It was better than any of my prescription drugs."

Now Betty stopped attending her regular Thursday night Bible study, and she no longer returned phone calls from friends. With nothing to interfere with her drinking, she progressed to three glasses of champagne a night. Occasionally she wondered if she was picking up a bad habit, but her fears always disappeared with her first drink.

One evening, only six months after she had started drinking, Betty unintentionally drank an entire bottle of champagne. She became violently sick and collapsed on the kitchen floor. Sometime in the middle of the night, feeling ashamed and afraid, she dragged herself to bed.

Very early the following morning, I felt prompted to call Betty and ask her if she had a drinking problem. It was a "divine coincidence." Since Betty's last physical, I had suspected that her lengthy grieving process might be a symptom of alcohol abuse.

"The call came so early, I didn't have any makeup on," remembers Betty. "Without that mask, it seemed easier to tell the truth. I regretted my honesty immediately, but then it was too late."

For the next three months, Betty tried a "controlled drinking experiment" with help from a local psychiatrist. Using a well-designed system of switching brands of wine and types of drinks, she attempted to limit herself to two drinks an evening. To her complete astonishment, she was never able to control the amount of alcohol she drank at any one sitting. She always drank until she was drunk.

Within a week after beginning the experiment, Betty's psychiatrist knew that she was an alcoholic. Betty herself was convinced that she could not be addicted after only six months of drinking, and she continued her efforts to control her consumption for three more months. Finally, she admitted that she was powerless over alcohol.

"It was just so unacceptable to me to be an alcoholic," recalls Betty. "After growing up with an alcoholic father and then watching my husband's suffering, I couldn't believe that it had happened to me."

Today, by following a spiritual program of recovery, Betty no longer drinks. She has returned to her Thursday night Bible study and eats dinner once a week with a "Single Again" fellowship at the Baptist church. She is separated from her six-month drinking spree by three years of sobriety, but occasionally she still feels an overwhelming urge for "one small drink." Such moments are an important reminder to Betty of the reality of her addiction: In just six months, she permanently crossed the line between moderate drinking and alcoholism.

One hundred million Americans drink alcoholic beverages; approximately ten million, like Betty Wilson, are alcoholics. These statistics hold true not just at cocktail lounges and in bars, but also at restaurants and private dinner parties. For every ten drinkers, there is likely to be at least one man, woman, or child who cannot control the amount of alcohol he or she consumes.

Why do some people become alcoholics while others are able to drink moderately all their lives? This is a question which has puzzled medical researchers and lay people for years. The most popular explanations are psychological. Social drinkers, it is said, exercise self-control; alcoholics suffer from weakness of will. "I can't believe he let himself get into that shape!" "Mary Anne can't hold her liquor." These frequently heard judgments question the alcoholic's character, implying that at best he lacks self-discipline; at worst, he is morally defective. In either case, the message is the same: "I would never let myself fall so far."

Biological or social explanations are less condemning. Many people believe that there are physical problems peculiar to alcoholics: allergies, liver disease, blood-sugar disorders, poor metabolism of alcohol, body chemistry imbalances—the list goes on. Sociologists, on the other hand, frequently focus on unhappy childhoods, broken homes, abusive parents. They speculate that emotionally deprived children become love-starved adults whose only comfort is found in a bottle.

None of these theories, however well-intended, is supported by research. In fact, in many cases, carefully conducted investigations not only have disproven such popular assumptions, but have shown their opposites to be true. For example:

1. *There is no alcoholic personality.* People who work with alcoholics know there are many personality traits which show up with uncommon frequency among ad-

dicted people. Alcoholics seem more dependent, more anxious, more childish, more oral (given to heavy smoking, compulsive talking, and eating), more self-centered, and less self-controlled than non-alcoholics. The presence of these psychological similarities has given rise to speculation that insecure and dependent people are more likely to become alcoholics than happy, well-adjusted, and independent-minded individuals.

However, a fascinating study conducted by Dr. George Vaillant at Harvard University confirms what many alcoholism counselors have long suspected: Whatever the common personality traits are among alcoholics, they develop after the onset of addiction, not before. Psychological similarities are a *consequence*, not a *cause* of addiction, and unstable people or those in chronic emotional pain are at no greater risk for developing alcoholism than their happy, well-adjusted neighbors.[1]

2. *Alcoholism has no known physical cause.* Many people have tried to prove through scientific experiments that there are discernible physical differences between alcoholics and non-alcoholics *prior to addiction*. So far, no one has succeeded. While researchers in brain neurochemistry are making substantial progress and may soon identify a specific physical problem common to all alcoholics, none of the popular notions about the causes of addiction have proven to be true. If alcoholics have allergies, blood-sugar disorders, vitamin deficiencies, or sick livers, it is a consequence of their drinking, not a cause.

3. *An unhappy childhood is not a primary cause of alcohol addiction.* Children from broken homes or with abusive parents are predictably at high risk for developing serious physical and mental problems as adults. However, a bad home life in and of itself does not increase a child's chances of developing alcoholism as an adult. Perhaps even more startling, children of alcoholic parents are not at high risk for developing alcoholism *simply* because they grow up in alcoholic homes. For every child from an alcoholic family who becomes an alcoholic in apparent response to his mother or father's drinking, there is per-

haps another child who avoids alcohol altogether as a
reaction against his parent's behavior.[2]

While there are no known psychological, physical, or
sociological problems common to all alcoholics, some of
us are at higher risk for developing an addiction than
others. In all of our lives, three major factors need close
examination:

1. *The Family Tree.* It is increasingly clear that alcoholism, or the potential for addiction, is passed from father to
son and from mother to daughter not because of bad
home environments, but because of family inheritance
patterns. The important role of heredity has been supported by several independent studies and recently received extraordinary confirmation from an investigation
of adopted children in Sweden, where adoption records
are traditionally well kept. Here, in one patient subgroup
studied, sons of alcoholic fathers placed *at birth* in non-
alcoholic families were found to have a nine-to-one
chance of becoming alcoholics over adopted sons born to
non-alcoholic parents. The mother to daughter transmission stood at three-to-one.[3]

Medical genetics is still in its infancy, but none of us
can afford to ignore these startling statistics. Perhaps it is
time for all of us to examine our family trees. Is there an
alcoholic in the house? Do we have a close relative—a
father, mother, uncle, aunt, grandparent, brother, or sis-
ter—with a drinking problem?

The average social drinker, we have learned, runs a
one-in-ten chance of developing an addiction to alcohol.
With an alcoholic in the family tree, social drinking takes
on a resemblance to Russian roulette. Thousands of alcoholics confirm Betty Wilson's story: Alcoholism is an unconscious drift towards addiction. By the time the geneti-
cally susceptible drinker is aware that he is in trouble, it is
too late. He is caught in an addiction from which he cannot return without help.

When we consider the subtle nature of addiction and
the infinite value of every individual life, uniquely created

by God for his special purpose, those of us who drink and have alcoholism in our family tree must ask a sensible question: Is it worth it? Are the rewards of alcohol so great that they balance out the risk of developing an incurable addiction? If the answer to this question is no, it is time to find an alternative method of relaxation. With a family history of addiction, total abstinence is a sensible, responsible approach to alcohol.*

2. *Crises.* John Swenson retired from his executive position in a textile plant at the age of sixty-five. The sudden transition from a prestigious, time-consuming job to endless, anonymous days of leisure left John feeling tired and depressed. A well-meaning friend advised him to liven up his day with "The Today Show" and a little vodka in his morning orange juice. John, who was never a regular drinker, began to down a screwdriver with his breakfast cereal.

Within less than a year, John was drinking a fifth of whiskey a day. By the time his concerned friend brought him to my office in a wheelchair, John was the sickest elderly alcoholic I had ever seen. It was two months before he was able to walk with a cane and enter a treatment center.

Retirement, business failure, illness, divorce, death. None of us is immune from personal crises, and during such periods, all of us are at significantly high risk for the development of alcohol addiction. Like Betty Wilson or John Swenson, we may be abstinent or moderate drinkers and suddenly find that a difficult experience tempts us to seek comfort in alcohol. At such critical times, regardless

---

* Parents who, in the presence of a family history of addictive drinking, are concerned about their children developing alcoholism should be aware that children of *dogmatic* teetotalers—those who continually make a major issue about drinking—are at unusually high risk for developing an addiction. An informative, nonalarmist approach is required. The "Letter to My Grandchildren" in Appendix A is one example of a positive approach to children at risk.

of our previous drinking habits and even in the absence of an inherited susceptibility, total abstinence should be given serious consideration.

3. *Culture.* "Drinking is the same all over the world." This was the informed judgment of a European alcoholism expert until he visited Gallup, New Mexico. There, on the border of a Navajo reservation, he found a town literally covered with alcoholics. Drunken Indians passed out on the street were almost as common as empty beer bottles scattered along the roadside. Eight hundred drunk arrests were made each month, and on any given night, up to two hundred inert Indians could be found sleeping off intoxication at a church shelter. "There is something horrifying about the look of Navajo drinking in Gallup," wrote Calvin Trillin. "Something that makes it less like big-city skid-row drinking than like a medieval epidemic."[4]

American Indians, Eskimos, the Irish, the French— these are only a few of the cultures in which alcoholism has long stood at epidemic proportions. The number of alcoholic Indians and Eskimos is a national tragedy, but it is the French who lay claim to the highest alcoholism rate. The average Frenchman consumes the equivalent of six to eight martinis a day, and 7 percent of all French people drink more than the equivalent of eighteen martinis a day.

At the opposite end of the spectrum are Moslems, Mormons, Jews, and Italians. Moslems and Mormons, who forbid the drinking of alcoholic beverages, have almost no alcoholism in their communities. Jews and Italians also have surprisingly low rates of alcoholism. Jews in particular are frequent subjects for study; even though few practice total abstinence, until recently, few developed alcoholism.[5]

What separates cultures with high rates of alcoholism from those with low rates? It is not, as is frequently supposed, biological or racial differences. The two most important factors are attitudes toward public drunkenness and whether or not drinking takes place outside of meals.

Nations and communities that drink only at the dinner table and do not tolerate public drunkenness do not have high rates of alcoholism.

When we examine American culture in light of these findings, the news is not encouraging. Americans habitually drink outside of meals and tolerate "party drunkenness" to such a degree that it is difficult to distinguish heavy drinkers from alcoholics. A medical student once told me, "There was no way my father could tell that my mother was an alcoholic because he was drinking so heavily himself." And an alcoholic patient said, "I never needed to conceal my drinking because all of my friends were doing the same thing; too much drinking at parties was not just socially acceptable, it was the in thing to do."

This cultural inclination toward excessive consumption of alcohol is no minor social problem. Heavy drinking is to alcoholism what smoking is to lung cancer—an effective, reliable means of developing a terminal illness. Even in the absence of a personal crisis or an inherited predisposition, heavy drinking can lead almost anyone at any time of life into alcoholism.

The connection between heavy drinking and addiction has profound implications not just for our society, but for each one of us individually. It brings us face to face with an important and personal question: How much is too much?

3

How Much Is Too Much?

"I know my limit." This is the bold claim made by heavy drinkers who consistently drink all their friends under the table. It is also said by social drinkers who stop at one or two drinks and by people who choose not to drink at all. Other people may have drinking problems, but we ourselves are certain we know when to quit.

Is there a safe amount of alcohol which a person can drink? It is a question for which there is no known answer. The amount of alcohol which will lead any given individual into addiction is impossible to determine; there are too many variables. Nonetheless, there are specific patterns which we would all do well to keep in mind.

1. *There are "instant addicts."* For reasons which are still unknown, there are some people who are profoundly affected by alcohol from their very first drink. Such people never have the opportunity to drink socially; they are immediately out of control of their drinking.

Marty Mann tells the story of one instant addict, an eighty-year old matriarch of a prominent New England family. Following her doctor's advice, this grandmother took her first drink at the age of seventy-nine and immediately began raiding the family liquor closet. "Terrible tales came back to plague the family pride—of mayhem in public bars, of teetering progress down the main street with a bottle tucked under each arm, of agitated policemen. . . . [The family] took the only possible out, and when last heard of the old lady was enjoying herself in a good sanitarium where the kindly doctors allowed her four drinks a day, and she spent her time conniving to get five or six."[1]

Instant addicts come in all ages, and while they are a minority, their number is greater than many of us would like to think. It is possible that these alcoholics come from families with a history of addiction, but at present this remains speculation.

2. *Heavy drinking, or frequent drunkenness, is a major factor in addiction.* A person who regularly drinks to the point of intoxication, or who drinks three or four drinks a day, three or more times a week, is placing himself or herself in a high risk category for developing alcoholism. *Even in the absence of an inherited predisposition,* this kind of drinking, over a period of seven to ten years, can lead anyone into addiction.

In the presence of a family history of alcoholism, heavy drinking takes on the character of a suicide wish. Sooner or later, it is likely to demand payment. With an alcoholic father, Betty Wilson became an addict in six months. Other people with alcoholism in their family tree drink for ten, twenty, or even thirty years before they lose control of their drinking.

With or without such a family history, heavy drinking is always high-risk drinking. No matter how many years a heavy drinker successfully avoids addiction, with each passing year, he increases his chances of becoming an alcoholic.

3. *There are no safe forms of alcohol.* The man who says he can't be an alcoholic because he only drinks beer is fooling himself, but not his liver. Some of the most badly damaged livers I've ever seen belonged to beer-aholics who were astonished to learn that they had been killing themselves with six-packs. These people were certain that drinking beer was less dangerous than drinking whiskey or vodka or even wine. The truth is that the alcohol content in one can of beer equals the alcohol con-

tent in a mixed drink or a glass of wine. The formula is easy to remember: one twelve-ounce can of beer = one six-ounce glass of wine = one mixed drink.

4. *There are no safe amounts of alcohol.* The amount of alcohol that any one person can drink without becoming intoxicated depends on size, sex, age, and metabolism rate. Betty Wilson was drinking "heavily" at two glasses of champagne a day, and I have known patients who were regularly intoxicated on one beer or a glass of wine.

Regardless of the kind or amount of alcohol consumed, and irrespective of whether addiction sets in instantly or over a period of many years, the end result is the same. Once a person is addicted to alcohol, he has set in motion forces over which he no longer has control. As the following story of Dr. Samuel Jackson illustrates, the alcoholic is trapped in a complex and finely woven web of despair.

4

Journey into Despair

Dr. Samuel Jackson was sixteen years old when he drank his first hard liquor. The year was 1941, Sam was a guest at a debutante ball, and the beverage was "home brew" mixed with fruit punch. After one drink, Sam's natural shyness seemed to disappear. After two drinks, he felt unusually witty and exceptionally graceful on the dance floor. By midnight, he was badly intoxicated. He drove himself and his friends home at dangerously high speeds, and in the morning he had a severe hangover. It seemed a small and grown-up price to pay for an evening of social success.

Fourteen years later, Sam was a well-established family doctor in a small midwestern city. He had married his high-school sweetheart and she was expecting the third of their four children. An active member in his local church, Sam took time from his busy practice to sing in the choir and teach a popular Sunday school class for teenagers. The pages of his Bible were well marked from hours of private study.

Since Sam's high school years, his drinking habits had changed several times. He joined the army at the age of eighteen, and for three years drank sporadically, but heavily. When the war ended, he went to college and spent Saturday nights drinking with fraternity brothers. In medical school, Sam stopped drinking altogether. In his early thirties, as a married man with a substantial income, he joined a country club and began drinking on weekends with golfing friends.

Over the next ten years, Sam increased his drinking to three or four times a week and occasionally became drunk on weekends. Sam's wife strongly opposed his drinking, and while Sam resented her interference, he frequently stopped drinking for months at a time.

In his early forties, Sam began to drink every day. He poured himself a drink as soon as he came home from work and frequently had two or three more drinks in the evening. His wife was alarmed by this change in his drinking habits and at one point left for several months. Because Sam valued his marriage more than his vodka, he substantially cut back on his drinking.

In 1976, Sam's wife was seriously injured in a car accident and was permanently bedridden with moderate brain damage. Sam was left alone to care for his wife, a nine-year-old son, a large house, and an enormous medical practice.

Burdened by loneliness and new responsibilities, Sam stepped up his drinking. Every evening he returned home from his hospital rounds, prepared dinner for his wife and son, and poured himself a large glass of vodka. He drank three or four glasses before going to bed and often fell asleep in the living room.

Within two years of his wife's accident, Sam was drinking more than a gallon of vodka a week. He became increasingly frightened by his heavy consumption and several times stopped drinking for weeks at a time. During these periods, his desire for alcohol was an overwhelming, almost physical presence in his life. At every waking moment, he was consciously *not* drinking. This minute-by-minute battle exhausted Sam's physical and mental resources, and when a television beer commercial or careless dose of cough syrup finally broke his resistance, Sam felt as if a victory had just been won. It was only when he was drinking that he could think about something other than alcohol.

By now, Sam was suffering from high blood pressure, chronic diarrhea, a stomach ulcer, arm and leg pain, and the morning "shakes." He could barely hold his tooth-brush, and every morning the taste of toothpaste caused him to vomit in the sink.

While mornings were difficult, days seemed endless. "You can't imagine the work it takes to be an alcoholic and carry on a demanding job," says Sam. "When I was working, I never drank before 5:30 in the evening, but I was always nauseated and sick and fighting a terrible desire to drink. I could hardly think, yet I had to function at an extremely high level."

Thanks to mentholated cough drops and a well-meaning medical partner, none of Sam's friends or patients knew he had a drinking problem. It was only during nighttime emergency calls that Sam began to slip noticeably. More than once he minimized the seriousness of a patient's condition so that he would not have to drive while intoxicated. If he was forced to go to the hospital, he frequently prescribed medications or made diagnoses of which he had no memory in the morning. He blamed his memory lapses on fatigue; sympathetic nurses and medical technicians covered for his mistakes. Meanwhile, in an attempt to reduce the frequency of his night driving, Sam worked hard to help establish a city emergency room that would handle night calls.

Despite his drinking, Sam felt an enormous responsibility for the welfare of his son, and he made an ongoing effort to be a good father. He served as president of the Pop Warner Football League, drove for the Little League car pool, and frequently took his son and his young friends roller-skating, although at times he could not remember the trip home.

Every Sunday Sam sent his son to church, but he himself no longer attended services. "It was just too painful," explains Sam. "I envied the people there, and I sincerely wanted to give my life to God, but it was no longer mine to give."

With no energy left for friends or dinner invitations, the single constant factor in Sam's life was guilt. "I despised myself. I felt guilty for drinking, for being an incompetent doctor, for being a bad father, and for hating everyone who in any way stood between me and what I needed most—a drink. I went through each day feeling like a wound-up spring. I wanted to hurt people, and I wanted to hurt myself for having such terrible feelings."

No matter how badly Sam felt about his drinking, he always knew there was a remedy. If he could just get to a bottle, after two drinks his anger and self-hatred melted away. "There were only fifteen or twenty minutes out of the day when I felt like a human being," remembers Sam. "That was between my second and third drink. Pain was an accepted way of life, and it had gone on for so long I never expected it to change. But at least for a few minutes every evening, life was bearable."

In January of 1981, in an unguarded moment, Sam agreed to sing in the church choir for a series of special meetings. Before each service, he became increasingly angry; his drinking was being delayed an average of three hours each night. After each service, he fought an overwhelming desire to confess his alcoholism to the church. "I wanted help so badly," says Sam. "But a voice in my head kept saying, 'Don't be a fool. You know you don't want to stop drinking. You can't imagine life without alcohol. If you tell them you're an alcoholic, everyone will know—but you will keep on drinking.'"

On the last night of the services Sam was hurrying out the door for a drink when he was stopped in the hall by a concerned friend. It was a woman whose elderly mother he had neglected during a night emergency call from the local nursing home. Now, this woman was troubled by Sam's sad appearance and asked about his wife. "My problem isn't my wife," Sam replied bluntly. "My problem is alcohol. I can't stop drinking."

Sam's unexpected confession led to a prayer service with the church elders, and Sam received an immediate desire to stop drinking. His craving for alcohol disappeared for a season. During this time, I met Sam at a church conference, heard his story, and directed him to a local support group for alcoholics.

Sam was convinced that he never again would be tempted to drink, but as a precautionary measure he went to the support group and made immediate friends. Several months later, from out of nowhere, his desire to drink returned with a terrible intensity. By then Sam was surrounded by a strong support system, and for the first time in his life, he resisted his craving for alcohol.

Today Sam is sober. His friends and patients wonder why he looks ten years younger, and Sam is still astonished to wake up every morning to the absence of pain. "My head doesn't hurt, my hands don't shake, and there is no boring pain in my stomach. I never thought I would feel this good again."

With God's help, Sam stays sober "one day at a time." "Alcohol is patient," Sam says. "It waits for you. As the months go by, things get easier, but a craving to drink still returns when I least expect it. From out of nowhere, I suddenly have an overwhelming desire for 'just one more drink.'"

Sam Jackson is one of an estimated thirteen to twenty-five thousand physicians in the United States who have permanently crossed the line between social drinking and alcoholism. These physicians, along with millions of other alcoholics, no longer drink to feel good; they drink to feel normal. In many cases, they are knowingly drinking themselves to death, but like Sam, they are more afraid of not drinking than of dying.

What is this strange and baffling disorder which causes so many of our best and brightest citizens to destroy themselves? A bad habit? A weakness in the will? A disease?

To answer these questions, it is helpful if we first digest a few basic facts about alcohol and the nature of addiction.

5

Abuse vs. Addiction

Alcohol, wrote George Bernard Shaw, "makes life bearable to millions of people who could not endure their existence if they were quite sober. It enables Parliament to do things at eleven at night that no sane person would do at eleven in the morning."[1]

For hundreds of years, alcohol has been the traditional "high" of Western culture. Its widespread use and acceptance, as well as its legality, have served to mask an important fact: Alcohol, our national social lubricant, is a drug.

Medically speaking, alcohol is an irregularly descending depressant of the central nervous system. In plain English, it interferes in progressive and predictable stages with the normal control functions of the brain.

In small amounts, often one drink or less, alcohol acts on that part of the brain which controls inhibitions. It relaxes or removes the restraints which govern behavior, giving the drinker a sense of euphoria and well-being. This release of the emotions from their normal controls, or *mood-altering* effect, frequently causes alcohol to be mislabeled as a stimulant. In fact, it is a depressant which slows down the intellect and other bodily functions.

In larger quantities, alcohol depresses the cerebellum and interferes with the body's balance mechanism. The drinker begins to stagger, and his speech becomes slurred.

Because his judgment is seriously impaired, the drinker is usually unaware that he can no longer properly walk—or drive. For most people, two and a half drinks (approximately three to four ounces of alcohol) in one hour is more than enough to make driving a risky business.

In very large quantities, alcohol anesthetizes the brain stem, the body's control center for respiration and heartbeat. A fifth of whiskey in an hour is normally enough to paralyze completely the brain stem and send the drinker into an alcoholic coma. This lethal effect of alcohol is generally unknown. Every year a number of high-school and college students are admitted dead-on-arrival to hospital emergency rooms because they accepted the challenge to chug-a-lug six-packs of beer or a fifth of vodka.

As a toxic drug which requires no digestion, alcohol is distributed uniformly throughout body tissues and cells. The rate of absorption depends on factors such as how much food is in the stomach and how much alcohol is in the beverage. The higher the concentration of alcohol, the more quickly the alcohol is absorbed by the body—whiskey has more "kick" than beer.

Alcohol is removed from the body primarily through the liver, the body's detoxification plant. The liver processes approximately one drink per hour: one mixed drink, one six-ounce glass of wine, or one twelve-ounce glass of beer. It cannot speed up this process. Consequently, if a person consumes two drinks in one hour, one drink continues to circulate through his body while his liver processes the other. Six drinks in one hour leaves the drinker intoxicated five hours later.

Why is alcohol addicting? No one really knows. Many drugs, such as morphine, are thought to "hook up" with specific receptors on the nerve cell wall, and there is some speculation that the same may be true for alcohol. There is also some evidence that long-term exposure to alcohol causes changes in nerve cell membranes, enabling them to function normally, even when saturated with alcohol. If this is true, it is possible that one day both withdrawal symptoms and "tolerance"—the ability to drink increasingly large amounts of alcohol—will be explained as a consequence of the nerve cell's ability to adapt to a toxic environment.[2]

Whatever the physiological basis of alcoholism may prove to be, alcohol addiction cannot be explained solely in terms of physical dependence. The alcoholic's physical need for alcohol, however binding, is inseparably connected to an equally powerful emotional dependence. Emotional dependence, as we saw in the story of Dr. Samuel Jackson, is rooted in the mood-altering properties of alcohol and affects every aspect of the human personality. It also enables us to distinguish, at least in theory, between people who are simply drinking too much and people who are genuinely alcohol-dependent.

The Alcohol Abuser

For most of his adult life, Dr. Samuel Jackson was not an alcoholic. He was a heavy drinker, an alcohol *abuser*. From the age of sixteen, when he first discovered the joys of intoxication, Sam rarely drank less than three or four drinks at a sitting. He enjoyed the mood-altering effect of heavy drinking, and as circumstances permitted, he drank more and more frequently.

Like most alcohol abusers, Sam could choose when he drank, how much he drank, or even if he drank. When his wife left him for several months, she raised the price of intoxication beyond that which he was willing to pay. The painful consequences of excessive drinking suddenly outweighed its pleasures, and Sam cut back on his consumption.

Thousands, perhaps millions, of alcohol abusers have similar experiences every year. A young girl drinks too much at a sorority party, vomits all over her dress, and wakes up in the morning with distressing memories. The brief euphoria of drunkenness is forgotten in the pain of social embarrassment, and she determines never to drink heavily again. Or a respected member of the community gets drunk on New Year's Eve, has an accident, and receives a "Driving While Intoxicated" citation. His family is angry, he pays a stiff fine, and he vows that he has had his last drink. That is the end of the problem.

The Alcohol Addict

For the alcohol addict, however, the problems never end. The alcoholic is an individual who cannot predict *when* he will drink or *how much* he will drink, and who continues to drink even after alcohol causes him trouble in one or more areas of his life—family, friends, health, job, finances, legal matters, and so on. Unlike the alcohol abuser, the alcohol addict is no longer in control of his own will. His internal center for decision-making and free choice has been captured by alcohol and he is unable to choose not to drink.

This loss of self-control is extremely difficult for social drinkers and abstainers to understand. It is tempting to dismiss alcoholism as a problem unique to weak-willed people, but the truth is that strong determination is no defense against addiction. I have watched more than one stubborn, strong-willed person involuntarily drink himself or herself to death, and the only significant difference I have ever noticed between strong and weak personalities is that strong-willed alcoholics pursue their drinking with more aggressive methods.

Because alcohol addiction is only one aspect—the extreme end—of the whole spectrum of alcohol abuse, it is impossible to determine exactly when heavy drinking ends and addiction begins. Sam Jackson was an alcohol abuser until his wife's accident. Shortly afterwards, he was an alcoholic. It took him over thirty years of heavy drinking to cross the line into addiction, but for all of his adult life, he was only a short step from trouble.

The euphoria that compels a heavy drinker to risk embarrassment or serious accident is only a distant memory for the alcoholic. The alcoholic still depends upon alcohol to alter his mood, but he drinks primarily to numb his pain, not to feel good. The constant physical agitation produced by his craving for alcohol combines with a paralyzing guilt and self-hatred to trap the alcoholic in a chronic state of mental anguish. Even the most lion-hearted of men and women cannot live in this state indefinitely. With relief as close at hand as the nearest liquor store, the alcoholic, whether he consciously chooses to drink or not, inevitably finds himself intoxicated.

Contrary to popular belief, it is not necessary to drink day and night to be an alcoholic. One of the most baffling forms of alcoholism is binge drinking, a form of addiction in which the drinker gets drunk weekly or monthly, but is sober many more days than he is drunk. Frequently, the period of time between binges becomes increasingly shorter, but this is not always the case. Even long-term alcoholics can experience periods of sobriety of up to two years or more, and many alcoholics periodically quit drinking to prove to their families and themselves that they are normal drinkers. Sooner or later, however, the test period ends, and the alcoholic is once again *involuntarily* drinking to intoxication.

Is Alcoholism a Disease—or a Sin?

When doctors and mental health workers refer to alcoholism as a disease, many people get understandably nervous. They see the disease label as a "humanistic" ploy, a modern attempt to deny the willful sinfulness of human beings and excuse the alcoholic from responsibility for his or her own behavior.

From the Christian perspective, alcohol abuse, or drunkenness, is clearly immoral. While contemporary Western society accepts intoxication within limits (it is all right to be drunk at a party, but not behind the wheel), the Bible forbids drunkenness altogether. The apostle Paul says:

> The acts of the sinful nature are obvious: sexual immorality, impurity and debauchery; idolatry and witchcraft; hatred, discord, jealousy, fits of rage, selfish ambition, dissensions, factions and envy; drunkenness, orgies, and the like. I warn you, as I did before, that those who live like this will not inherit the kingdom of God (Gal. 5:19–21).

It's not hard to understand why Paul speaks so strongly. Alcohol abuse is involved in most murders, most assaults, most child abuse cases, most traffic fatalities, and most fire and drowning accidents. It is also a primary factor in the development of alcohol *addiction*. For both reasons, we do ourselves and our entire society a great disservice when we laugh at drunkenness or treat it lightly.

While the alcohol abuser chooses to get drunk, the alcoholic drinks involuntarily. His will power is in service to his addiction and he cannot resist his craving for alcohol. Telling an alcohol addict to shape up and stop drinking is like telling a man who jumps out of a nine-story building to fall only three floors. Words will not alter the inevitable outcome.

Because of the alcoholic's helplessness, and because addiction follows a predictable pattern and has a pronounced inheritance factor, it is not inappropriate to call alcoholism a disease. However, it is never simply a *physical* disease; rather, alcoholism is the paradigm disease of the *whole* person. While an individual with diabetes or cancer can possess a healthy mind and emotions, and deep friendships and family ties, the alcoholic, more often than not, loses everything. He is sick in his body, mind, emotions, spirit, and relationships. Unless the alcoholic gets help in all four areas, his chances for recovery are very poor indeed.

"First the man takes a drink, then the drink takes a drink, then the drink takes the man." This ancient proverb says it well. Whatever label we attach to alcoholism, addiction has a life of its own. The alcoholic has set in motion powerful forces over which he has no control, and he begins to exhibit predictable but often unrecognized symptoms of addiction.

6

Warning Signs

"The earlier the diagnosis, the better the prognosis." This is a simple medical principle which applies to alcoholism as aptly as it does to cancer or heart disease. Statistically speaking, the earlier we identify the addiction problem, the more likely it is that the alcoholic will recover.

The opposite is also true. The longer we wait to diagnose alcoholism, the poorer the alcoholic's chances for recovery. Alcohol addiction is a progressive, chronic, and comprehensive disorder. If left to run its course, it gets worse, not better. The longer an alcoholic drinks, the more completely he destroys himself. When he has finally lost everything—his personality, family, friends, health, and job—the alcoholic is terminally ill and has little incentive for living, much less staying sober.

The importance of recognizing the early warning signs of addiction cannot be overemphasized. Unfortunately, the best known symptoms of alcoholism are physical problems which occur in the late stages of addiction: a red face, a bulbous nose, cirrhosis of the liver. Less understood, but vastly more important, are the specific behavior problems and early physical warning signs of addiction. Not every alcoholic manifests every possible symptom, but there is a predictable pattern of behavior which can be recognized by alert family members, friends, and employers or employees.

The Sickness of the Spirit

Long before a heavy drinker becomes an alcoholic, his relationship with God is badly damaged. Heavy drinking quenches spiritual understanding and often leads the drinker to violate his own moral principles. As a mood-altering drug, alcohol acts directly on the cerebrum to depress or remove our built-in prohibitions against certain kinds of behavior. We are all far more dependent upon these inhibitions than we want to believe, and without them we are subject to control by the specific weaknesses of our own particular character—anger, self-pity, greed, hatred, violence, lust, and so on.

A man or woman with perfectly fine family values might drink too much, become euphoric, and climb into bed with a casual acquaintance. When the alcohol wears off, he or she is left with deep feelings of guilt and shame. If the wrongdoing goes unconfessed, the feelings of shame are suppressed, but the memory is very much alive. This memory continually chips away at the drinker's already damaged moral life.

For the alcoholic, the moral damage never ends. He repeatedly violates his own sense of right and wrong by telling petty lies, cheating at work, hiding bottles, stealing, and verbally or physically abusing other members of his family. In cases closer to home than many of us realize, alcoholics also commit rape, incest, and murder.

However twisted and unpredictable the actions of the alcoholic become, his conscience is never fully soluble in alcohol. He is aware of his moral corruption, and he is tormented by guilt. "It is impossible to describe the emotional pain experienced by an alcoholic," says Dr. Samuel Jackson. "No matter how arrogant or self-confident he may seem, his primary emotions are shame and self-hatred."

Under this strong sense of condemnation, most alcoholics drop out of church. They dismiss church members as hypocrites, although they may secretly envy their appearance of respectability. A few alcoholics continue to attend

religious services, but no matter how sincerely they seek
to serve God, their spirituality is devoid of power.

No alcoholic can survive indefinitely the spiritual isolation and self-hatred generated by addiction. A phenom-
enal number of alcoholics eventually choose to kill themselves; their suicide rate is thirty times greater than that
of the general population. The vast majority of alcoholics,
however, survive long enough to drink themselves to
death. To do so, they must make use of the sophisticated
defense system by which the damaged human mind pro-
tects itself from collapse.

The Sickness of the Mind and Emotions

Very early in the addictive process, the alcoholic moves
from *anticipation* to *preoccupation* with drinking. He no
longer simply looks forward to drinking; he thinks about
it all the time. His mental and emotional energies are almost completely directed at protecting his right to drink
and living with his declining self-esteem. Accordingly, he
begins to manifest predictable symptoms.

Rationalization and Projection. "I always had a con-
vincing reason to drink," remembers a forty-five-year-old
alcoholic patient. "First I drank to be social. Then I drank
to relax after work. Next I drank to sleep. Finally I drank
to forget. None of these explanations seemed to be rationalizations at the time. I had real needs, and I was convinced that only alcohol could meet them."

As the alcoholic's addiction progresses, his need for alcohol increases. He begins to drink more and more frequently and plans his entire day around his drinking
schedule. He often hides bottles at home or at work and
becomes extremely irritated when unexpected schedule
changes force him to delay his drinking.

As the alcoholic's behavior grows increasingly *rigid,* his
rationalizations often become more and more pathological. Through subtle criticism or shocking accusations, he
projects his self-hatred onto the people closest to him. He
may blame his drinking on his wife's nagging, his chil-

dren's ungratefulness, or his employer's unfairness. Often the alcoholic's accusations become so twisted and ugly that family relationships and friendships are permanently damaged or destroyed.

The alcoholic has an uncanny ability to convince other people that they are responsible for his drinking, and it is family members who are most vulnerable to his accusations. Pushed to the breaking point by the alcoholic's unpredictable behavior, many wives or husbands of alcoholics seek psychiatric help—for themselves. One wife of an alcoholic spent three months in a mental institution before counselors discovered that she was there because her husband had convinced her she was crazy.

Mood Swings and Personality Changes. While the alcoholic is increasingly critical of the people around him, his own behavior is, at best, unpredictable. He becomes irritable and defensive, and his mood can change from jubilant euphoria to angry suspicion in a matter of minutes. These mood swings are particularly pronounced when the alcoholic is "on the wagon" or attempting to cut back on his drinking.

At the extreme end of mood swings is the *Dr. Jekyll and Mr. Hyde syndrome.* For reasons not yet known, some people undergo a complete personality change when they are drinking. This transformation closely resembles the presence of two personalities in one body, and for family members, it is one of the most terrifying aspects of alcoholism. A father, mother, husband, wife, or child disappears, and in his or her place is a total stranger who is often devoid of conscience.

One of my alcoholic patients was a highly moral man who, while he was drinking, watched pornographic movies in front of his children. Another patient, a bank executive and prominent church member, was unusually considerate and charming to his family until he had a few drinks. Then anything could happen. Once he spent a European vacation roaming up and down the streets in his underwear and knocking on doors, challenging the local residents to a fight. His children hid behind a barricaded door, fearful that he would make good his threats to return and kill them.

The bizarre nature of the Dr. Jekyll and Mr. Hyde syndrome leads many people to speculate that alcoholism is a consequence of demon possession, that there is a "spirit" of alcoholism which invades alcoholics. Anyone who has witnessed firsthand an alcohol- or drug-induced personality change cannot dismiss this possibility lightly. My own opinion is that whenever we voluntarily surrender our inhibitions, the God-given fences which control our character weaknesses, we open ourselves up to the possibility of control by hostile spiritual forces. As a Christian, I do not want to underestimate Satan's ability to take advantage of human vulnerability. At the same time, I do not want to underestimate the toxic effects of chronic drinking. Even apart from "spiritual possession," alcohol and other drugs are powerful enough to produce schizophrenic personality changes in human beings.

Blackouts. Many alcoholics experience periods of time in which they function normally, never lose consciousness, and yet have no memory of where they were or what they did. These chemically-induced periods of amnesia are called *blackouts*. Sermons have been preached, cross-continental jets flown, heart surgery performed, and military operations executed by people who have no memory of any of the events which transpired. "When I remember the many nights I made diagnoses or prescribed drugs in an alcoholic blackout," says Dr. Samuel Jackson, "I know it's only by the grace of God that I never killed anyone."

Other alcoholics are not so fortunate. In his book *I'll Quit Tomorrow,* Dr. Vernon Johnson recalls an early morning phone call from a real estate broker. "They tell me that last night I drove my car through three kids on bicycles and killed one," the broker said in a dazed voice. "I don't remember. . . ." It was a lost memory with which the broker could not live. The night before his trial, he killed himself.[1]

The exact physical mechanism of blackouts is unknown, although it is thought to relate to alcohol's damaging effect on the chemical storage of short-term memories. The time frame covered by a memory loss can be minutes—or months. One alcoholic, a corporation executive, spent a week at a convention center, drinking and conducting high-level financial transactions. She returned to her home office only to discover that she had no memory of any agreements that she had made during the week. Another patient, a professor, has only a handful of memories from the last twenty years of his life.

Social Symptoms. The alcoholic frequently begins his drinking career as "the life of the party." By the time his addiction has progressed to recognizable stages, however, his old friends have usually disappeared. The intoxicated behavior of the alcoholic is no longer amusing as he becomes increasingly critical and angry toward non-alcoholics. The alcoholic narrows his social circle to people with whom he can drink heavily without embarrassment. If he is forced to attend a party where alcohol is not served, usually he has several drinks beforehand to fortify himself for the ordeal.

The family life of the alcoholic, for reasons which we will examine later, is usually hidden from the public eye. However, as his drinking continues, the alcoholic often complains of marriage problems, sexual frustrations, and financial difficulties. Sometimes there are sudden or unexplained changes in the family structure, such as separation or divorce, or children leaving home at early ages to live with relatives.

Although friends and family members experience the alcoholic's strange behavior early in his addiction, the alcoholic takes great pains to conceal his problem at work. Sooner or later, however, his job performance begins to deteriorate. He shows up late for work on Monday mornings or after holidays and has an increased number of unexplained absences. He finds it hard to concentrate for extended periods of time, and he may become increasingly moody or aggressive toward his fellow workers. Often, both the quantity and the quality of the alcoholic's work production fall to substandard levels.

Physical Symptoms. While the earliest symptoms of alcoholism are behavior patterns, it is not long before the alcoholic begins to pay a physical price for his addiction. Early physical symptoms include night sweats, morning nausea and vomiting, diarrhea, gastritis (inflammation of the stomach lining), hand tremors, a slightly enlarged or tender liver, and in men, impotence. Frequently, the alcoholic also has unexplained bruises or cigarette burns on his body.

As the alcoholic's addiction progresses, his physical problems become more serious. His face flushes, his nose often becomes inflamed and enlarged, his palms may turn red ("liver palms"), and he can suffer from any one of dozens of medical complications: high blood pressure, ulcers, pancreatitis, heart disease, cirrhosis, kidney failure, shrunken testicles, cancer of the esophagus, anemia, tuberculosis, irreparable brain damage, and so on. A complete list of alcohol-related medical problems reads much like a summary of everything that can go wrong with the human body.

By the late stages of addiction, the alcoholic's central nervous system has adjusted to the constant presence of alcohol. If his blood-alcohol level drops unexpectedly, he experiences withdrawal symptoms: rapid pulse, severe headaches, the shakes (involuntary trembling of the head, limbs, and tongue), and finally, *delirium tremens.* This "pink elephant" stage, despite its humorous reputation, is a nightmarish phenomenon which kills 15 percent of its victims. The alcoholic is mentally and physically tortured by his poisoned, malfunctioning brain, and often sees terrifying visions. One of my alcoholic patients was convinced for hours that he was being attacked by monstrous dogs leaping from tree limbs. Nothing could persuade him otherwise.

In the final stages of addiction, the alcoholic often suffers permanent brain damage. Years of heavy drinking have depleted his supply of thiamine, a vitamin necessary for growth and maintenance of nerve tissue, and his brain becomes diseased and shrinks in size. Two of the most common forms of alcohol-related brain disease are *Wernicke's syndrome* and *Korsakoff's psychosis*. Wernicke's syndrome is often reversible by injections of thiamine. Korsakoff's psychosis puts the alcoholic on skid row or in a nursing home.

With his health deteriorating, his personality crumbling, his job in jeopardy, and all his relationships heading to ruin, the alcoholic is desperately in need of help. Strangely, the longer his addiction continues and the bigger the price he pays for drinking, the less able he is to see himself as sick.

7

Don't Call Me an Alcoholic!

It was during John Morgan's sixth visit to his psychiatrist that he heard the good news. He was not an alcoholic. "You're badly depressed," the psychiatrist told him. "But give yourself time. Work things out with your wife and try not to drink so much."

John was relieved. It was good to hear a professional confirm what he had tried to tell his wife for months. The psychiatrist gave him some tranquilizers and a prescription for an antidepressant drug, and John headed back to work. Since it was Saturday, he stopped off at a local bootlegger for a half-pint to last through the weekend. The bottle was gone in an hour, and John drove back for more.

By four o'clock the same afternoon, John was playing golf with friends and working on his third half-pint. He played two holes and passed out on the third green. When he woke up, his friends were gone and it was raining. John was too embarrassed to return to the pro shop, so he staggered back to his truck. Underneath the seat was a warm bottle of vodka.

The next thing John knew it was Sunday afternoon, and the police were on the phone, notifying him that he owed the county eighteen dollars for a stop sign. John found a new dent on his truck and paid the fine without an argument; as a prominent businessman, he tried to keep his relationship with the police cordial. In fact, more than once he had driven the chief of police home when the chief was too intoxicated to drive.

John Morgan was a Bible college graduate, a former minister and radio preacher, and a successful antique auctioneer. He had been drinking alcoholically for thirteen years. His decision to leave the ministry had come immediately after the first drinking episode of his adult life. "From the very beginning, I was unusually affected by alcohol," remembers John. "I knew right away I had to choose between serving God and drinking, and I chose to drink. Afterward, I tried to reestablish my relationship with God, but the damage was done. I'd get drunk, cry out to God for forgiveness, and promise never to drink again. Then the next thing I'd know, I'd have a bottle in my hand. This went on so long, I finally figured God didn't want any more of my business."

John was a binge drinker; his drinking episodes were separated by weeks, and sometimes even months. He often drank while traveling, and once he accidentally set a hotel on fire. He had been in fourteen different jails up and down the East Coast, and his driver's license was suspended or restricted almost every six months.

When John reached his early forties, his drinking pattern began to reverse itself. He stayed drunk for weeks at a time, sobering up only for auctions. When he wasn't drinking, he was a thoughtful husband and a kind father; when drunk, he was unpredictable and dangerous. Once he hit his wife and broke her nose. On another occasion he challenged his son to a fist fight. He even began to abuse his clients—threatening them with lawsuits, ordering customers out of the auction room, and smashing sale items on the platform.

John's wife, Linda, became increasingly frightened by his behavior. She tried to tell his family about his drinking, but John had already explained to them that it was his wife who drove him to the bottle. "He wasn't drinking when you married him," the family said. "When we gave him to you he was a preacher." Feeling more and more guilty, Linda tried to explain John's drinking to a church friend, an older woman whose insight she respected. Before she finished her story, she could see her friend did not believe her. "I'm exaggerating," Linda admitted. "It isn't that bad."

John's drinking grew progressively worse, and Linda went to the family doctor. She told him that John was an alcoholic. "He's not drinking that much," the doctor assured her. "Your nerves are acting up." He offered to give Linda a prescription for tranquilizers.

In 1974, Linda began to attend Al-Anon, a grassroots support group for family members and friends of alcoholics. When John found out, he was furious. "Are you trying to ruin our reputation?" he asked. "We have a business to run, and we can't afford this kind of publicity. Everyone in town will think I am an alcoholic!"

Linda kept going to Al-Anon, and one afternoon, in a state of sober depression, John agreed to attend Alcoholics Anonymous. By evening he was drunk, and when he became disruptive at the AA meeting, he had to be escorted outside. Still, he went back to three more meetings. Someone gave him a copy of AA's "Blue Book," and he spent his nights in front of the television, drinking and reading the testimonials of recovering alcoholics. "I liked to analyze their stories and figure out where they went wrong," John remembers. "I thought if I could avoid their mistakes, then I wouldn't become an alcoholic."

It was during this time that John went to a psychiatrist. "He wanted to know my habits when I was five years old," says John, "but I could hardly remember what I had done in the previous five days. I was so afraid he was going to tell me I was an alcoholic that I usually had a few drinks before our meetings to help me relax. You can't imagine how relieved I was to learn I didn't have a drinking problem. All I needed was a few pills for depression."

In the next year, John's addiction reached frightening proportions. He spent the two weeks prior to his eldest daughter's wedding in an alcoholic blackout—he lived in a hotel room, functioned normally, yet had no memory of over ten days of his life. He sobered up in time for the wedding but had to stiff-arm it through *delirium tremens*.

For hours John watched disfigured men crawling out of the walls, laughing and shrieking and offering him pints of vodka.

Two weeks after the wedding, John was back in a hotel room for another ten-day blackout. When he came to, he called his wife, begged for help, and agreed to enter a treatment center where Linda had already made reservations.

After two days of detoxification, and within three days of his admission to the treatment program, John was convinced he wasn't an alcoholic. "I became a counselor instead," John remembers. "Some of those people were really hurting, and my heart went out to them. Because of my ministerial background, many patients looked to me for spiritual expertise, and I was only too happy to help them."

In the third week of his treatment, one of John's "patients," a twenty-one-year-old woman, suffered a dramatic setback: She had been discharged from the treatment center with an optimistic prognosis, but was drunk before she reached her own doorstep. When John heard the news, he was devastated. He went to his room, pulled a chest of drawers in front of his door, and lay down on his bed. "I couldn't stop crying," John remembers. "My ego was shattered. What had I done wrong? How could God let this happen to a helpless young girl?"

John cried and prayed for six hours. "It was as if I was in an alcoholic blackout. When I came to, I was lying under my bed, weeping. I always told myself I was only crazy when I was drinking, but now I hadn't had a drink for twenty-one days. And all of a sudden I knew I was insane. What sane person would blockade the door and lie under the bed crying at three o'clock in the morning because someone else had gotten drunk? When I asked myself that question, everything I heard since beginning treatment became a reality. I was an alcoholic. My life was completely unmanageable, and I was powerless over my addiction. Unless God helped me, I would drink until I was dead."

For the first time since he started drinking, John

wanted to be sober more than he wanted to be drunk. He asked God to take control of his life, and he vowed he would do whatever was necessary to get well.

Since that night, John's craving for alcohol has never returned. He is an active member of Alcoholics Anonymous, and he and his wife work together in an alcoholism treatment program. "I used to promise my wife I'd never drink again," says John. "She heard enough promises to last a lifetime. Now, I don't make promises; we both just live one day at a time, giving our lives to God and trusting him to direct our paths."

John Morgan lost control of his drinking in 1963. For fourteen years he suffered serious public and personal consequences from his alcoholism, and for fourteen years he denied he had a drinking problem. He was supported in his self-deception by his family doctor, his psychiatrist, his church, and most of his family. This merry-go-round of denial, far from being unusual, is one of the most typical and tragic aspects of alcoholism.

It is the rare alcoholic who recognizes that he has lost control of his drinking. "I knew I was an alcoholic," admitted one fifty-seven-year-old patient, "but I didn't see any way out. I gave up thinking my life could ever be different, and I tried to appear to my family and friends as if I wasn't addicted."

The majority of alcoholics are not pretending when they deny their addiction. Whatever hopeless awareness exists at a subconscious level, they consciously believe that they are normal drinkers. The typical alcoholic can sit in a doctor's office dead drunk, with a swollen red nose and a liver falling down to his pelvic brim, and seriously claim to be a social drinker. One of my patients spent his mornings kneeling in front of a commode, vomiting up blood and intermittently drinking from a can of beer. As far as he was concerned, he didn't have a drinking problem.

For some alcoholics, denial takes more subtle forms. The compliant alcoholic periodically admits to his family or friends that he is "a no-good drunk," and begs for help and understanding. Sometimes he promises never to drink again. Sometimes he simply asks to be loved and accepted despite his human weakness. At such moments, the alcoholic is usually extremely persuasive—and extremely drunk. He has no genuine understanding of his addiction and no intention of giving up his bottle. His motivation, however unconscious, is to capture the sympathy of his audience and to discourage any effort to interfere with his drinking.

"I can quit when I want." "I don't drink as much as Harry." "I'll stop next year." These are the standard delusions of the alcoholic, and the longer he drinks, the more pronounced his denial becomes. It is not unusual for a man or woman lying in a hospital bed, dying of alcohol-induced cirrhosis, to assert confidently that he or she has never swallowed even so much as a single drink.

How can the alcoholic ignore the obvious consequences of his drinking and repeatedly deny his addiction? The full answer to this perplexing question is not yet known, but it is possible to identify some important contributing factors.

8

The Supporting Cast

Ever since Adam and Eve hid from God in the garden, human beings have been prone to self-deception. We delay facing unpleasant truths about ourselves as long as possible and often refuse to admit even our most obvious weaknesses.

In many cases, honest self-assessment begins only *after* we have paid a substantial price for our delusion. When the painful consequences of our actions outweigh the pleasure they bring us, we suddenly find ourselves giving serious thought to changing our behavior.

Patients suffering from high blood pressure are a case in point. High blood pressure, or hypertension, is a serious, life-threatening disease. It is also usually painless. Because patients with high blood pressure seldom feel sick, they commonly ignore their doctor's repeated warnings about diet, exercise, and proper medications. It is often only when they suffer painful consequences—a heart attack, stroke, severe headaches, kidney failure, partial blindness—that they take seriously their doctor's advice. Unfortunately, by then the damage is often irreparable.

Alcoholics behave in much the same way. They suffer from an overpowering craving for alcohol and the firm conviction that they cannot live without drinking. The longer their addiction continues, the stronger their craving becomes, and the fewer resources they possess for resisting temptation. Unless the painful consequences of drinking *clearly* outweigh its known benefits, the alcoholic will never surrender his right to drink.

As miserable as most alcoholics may seem, in most cases, they are not miserable enough. The alcoholic is sheltered from some of the most disturbing and painful results of his drinking by: (a) the chemical effects of alcohol on his judgment and memory; (b) his sophisticated system of psychological defense mechanisms; and (c) the well-intentioned efforts of the people closest to him—his doctor, minister, employer or employees, family, and friends.

Chemical Damage to Judgment and Memory

The toxic effects of alcohol seriously impair the alcoholic's ability to judge the appropriateness of his own actions. With his inhibitions removed and his mood temporarily elevated, the alcoholic can interpret even his most embarrassing and harmful actions as episodes of special insight and social success. Since drunkenness is often the single remaining pleasure in his life, the alcoholic recalls his intoxicated moments in a rosy, bucolic light. This *euphoric recall* conceals from the alcoholic the true nature of his behavior, and he is often surprised to discover that relationships have been permanently broken by actions which he remembers as unusually witty or clever.

The alcoholic's ability to learn from his mistakes is further damaged by chemically-induced memory blackouts. As illustrated in Chapter 7, some of the alcoholic's most shocking and reprehensible actions leave no memory trace in his brain. "He acts as if nothing happened," says the confused wife of an alcoholic, after a nightmarish evening of fighting. "Am I making the whole thing up?" Often, the truth is that, for the alcoholic, nothing *did* happen. While his wife is left to doubt her sanity and cope with searing memories of physical and verbal abuse, the alcoholic is cut off from vital feedback about his behavior by the chemical impairment of his memory. He has nothing to forget, because there is nothing he remembers.

Repression

In every life there are some events which are too painful or shameful to dwell on indefinitely. "If a fifty-year-old man could and did remember in a single moment of time *all* his shameful and painful acts in a half-century of living, he would go into an irreversible emotional collapse," says Dr. Vernon Johnson. "He simply could not bear such a burden—it would turn him into a gibbering idiot. . . ."[1]

In an attempt to live with the burden of past mistakes and wrongdoing, even the healthiest of human beings repress bad memories. *Repression* is the act of burying past events and actions so deeply that they are removed from conscious thought. This burial is an *automatic defense mechanism* of the wounded human psyche, and it takes place without conscious awareness.

For the alcoholic, repression is a full-time job. He constantly repeats the same immoral or humiliating acts, and usually his behavior deteriorates. In order to preserve his shaky self-esteem and his right to drink, the alcoholic must distance himself from his own actions. He represses his memories deep in his subconscious where he hopes they will do no further harm, but where in reality they fuel feelings of self-hatred and increase his need for alcohol. The alcoholic can become so adept at repression that he can convince himself in minutes he did not say or do the things from which he still suffers obvious consequences.

Enabling

Afflicted by memory distortions and armed with well-developed defense mechanisms, the alcoholic is trapped within a cage that has few openings from the inside. He cannot spontaneously recognize his addiction, and he is dependent upon other people to help him escape his delusion.

Sadly, the people closest to the alcoholic often become the supporting cast for his addiction. Despite their good intentions, doctors, ministers, employers, family members, and friends frequently enable the alcoholic to continue drinking by accepting his distorted version of reality and sheltering him from the painful consequences of his conduct. This enabling dynamic springs from our instinctive impulse to comfort and protect sick people, but for the alcoholic, whose one lifeline to sobriety is honest self-confrontation, it has disastrous consequences.

The Missed Diagnosis. Helen M. was married to a physician. She drank alcoholically for eleven years, during which time her desperate husband took her to eight psychiatrists and five consulting doctors. On different occasions she was labeled diabetic, hypothyroid, hypercholesterolemic, and Addisonian. One year she was hospitalized ten times for "unusual symptoms."

It was Helen's ninth psychiatrist who finally made the diagnosis. "I can't do a thing for you," he told Helen. "You're a drunk. Why don't you get into AA?"[2]

Almost every alcoholic and his family have a similar story to tell. The average alcoholic visits his doctor three times a year, complaining of headaches, depression, night sweats, high blood pressure, diarrhea, and marriage problems. Rarely, if ever, does he complain of alcoholism. His goal is to conceal his addiction and get treatment for his symptoms so that he can continue drinking without physical pain.

The vast majority of doctors are all too ready to cooperate with the alcoholic. Because only 3 percent of medical students take a course on alcoholism[3]—our nation's number three health problem—the average doctor or psychiatrist recognizes only the late-stage symptoms of addiction. When confronted with the vague physical and psychological complaints of the alcoholic, the doctor responds as he or she has been trained—and writes a prescription for tranquilizers or other mood-altering drugs.

With this simple gesture, every year thousands of doctors and psychiatrists help perpetuate the addiction of their alcoholic patients. Mood-altering drugs easily substitute for one another, and pills only further distort the alcoholic's already twisted perceptions. Like a good stiff drink, they enable the alcoholic to satisfy his craving and cope with the anxiety produced by his addiction. "My psychiatrist gave me sleeping pills, tranquilizers, and anti-depressants," remembers John Morgan. "Who needs alcohol with a deal like that?"

Because mood-altering drugs are interchangeable, a man or woman addicted to one drug, such as alcohol, easily becomes "cross-addicted" to another. Cross-addicted alcoholics have a substantially lower recovery rate than alcoholics in general, and they are more likely to die from an accidental overdose or suffer irreparable brain damage.*

It Couldn't Happen in Our Church! Joan was a Sunday school teacher, the vice-president of the Women's Circle, and a Sunday-morning hostess. She was also a leader in the charismatic renewal movement within her church, and she helped many members come to a deeper understanding of the gifts of the Holy Spirit.

When Joan's teenage children entered a rebellious stage and her husband's work kept him out late at night, Joan began to drink an occasional nightcap. Within a year from her first drink, she was downing a quart of Jack Daniels a day. For five years Joan drank alcoholically, experienced blackouts, carried on violent arguments with her husband—and never missed a meeting of her small charismatic prayer group. The fellowship she experienced among Christian believers enabled her to survive emotionally from one week to the next and, despite the intimate sharing which took place, no one in the group knew that Joan was addicted to alcohol. Her friends accepted her explanation that she was depressed and only learned

---

*It is important to note that mood-altering pills and alcohol are a potentially lethal combination for anyone, not just the alcoholic. Teenagers in particular need to be warned that drugs and alcohol, when taken together, have a *synergistic* effect— the total impact of their mix is greater than the sum of their parts. Quantities of pills or alcohol which might be safe when taken by themselves can cause permanent brain damage or death when ingested together.

of Joan's alcoholism after she had become a recovering alcoholic.

Perhaps you are saying, "It couldn't happen in *our* church." It can happen in any church, but it is the rare congregation that knows the extent of its drinking problem. Because church members often fail to distinguish between drunkenness and addiction, and because alcoholics are viewed in a judgmental and moralistic light, many Christians mistakenly believe that their fellow believers are immune from the danger of addiction. This conviction allows them to overlook even the most obvious symptoms of alcoholism, particularly if they appear in a Sunday school teacher, a deacon, or a minister.

The Christian alcoholic often shares the judgmental attitude of his fellow believers, and although he denies his addiction, he is secretly convinced that God has permanently rejected him. His own behavior appalls him. When he repeatedly drinks too much, and perhaps beats his wife, urinates on himself, or spends the night passed out in his own vomit, he is violating not just social codes, but spiritual principles which he knows to be God-ordained. The dissonance between belief and action is even more pronounced in alcoholic ministers, who may participate in all kinds of uncontrolled behavior during the week, but must preach from the pulpit on Sunday morning.

It is tempting to dismiss Christian alcoholics as hypocrites, but the guilt and shame they feel are far removed from the arrogant self-complacency condemned by Jesus. At the same time, the spiritual anguish of the alcoholic is seldom redemptive. He may have repented of drinking more times than he can remember, but because he cannot imagine life without alcohol, his confession never leads to a changed life. His spiritual beliefs only increase his sense of condemnation and compel him to adopt increasingly extreme denial measures.

Armed with the strong conviction that he is not an addict, the Christian alcoholic frequently visits his pastor or church leaders to complain of marriage problems, financial difficulties, or depression. Since his addiction remains concealed, the alcoholic is allowed to ventilate his feelings without doing anything about his underlying problem. He and his family learn practical tips for weathering their domestic crises, and pressures which might otherwise force the alcoholic to admit his addiction are effectively reduced. Often the Christian alcoholic becomes emotionally dependent upon his pastor or counselors, and this umbrella of external authority further reduces his sense of responsibility for his own actions.

On the Job, "He's Not a Bad Fellow." In 1959, Dr. Joseph Cruse wrecked his automobile while driving under the influence of alcohol. As a professional courtesy, his emergency room doctor "lost" the results of his blood-alcohol test. For the next eleven years, and through six hospital admissions, Dr. Cruse's colleagues ignored his intoxicated behavior and falsified his medical records. On his sixth admission to the hospital, a self-inflicted stab wound from a suicide attempt was labeled "an accidental cut."

"They covered up for me because I'm a buddy—a colleague," recalls Dr. Cruse, now a recovering alcoholic and former medical director of the Betty Ford Center for alcohol and drug addiction. "They did it with the best of intentions. But if they hadn't covered it up the first time, when I had the auto accident, somebody possibly could have saved me and my family eleven years of unhappiness."[4]

Conservative estimates place the number of alcoholic workers in the United States at 6 percent of the work force. These men and women cost their employers and business associates over fifteen billion dollars a year, and they are responsible for a tragic number of work-related accidents. Despite their declining productivity and the ever-present threat of a serious mishap, alcoholic employees are kept on the job by their fellow workers or employers who tolerate or cover up for their addiction.

What accounts for this almost universal effort to protect the alcoholic employee? Many alcoholics are bright, capable people who, even when functioning at half-speed, are more qualified than their peers. By the time their addiction surfaces, they often have worked at their job for years and have established close friendships and personal ties with their fellow workers. These friends are neither immune from the alcoholic's manipulative skills, nor do they wish to see him and his family lose their source of income.

The alcoholic's fellow employees or business associates often help him keep his job at great personal cost to themselves. They work extra hard to make up for his low productivity, cover up for his absences, and pick up the pieces after his most serious mistakes. Unfortunately, these well-intentioned efforts enable the alcoholic to continue drinking without paying the price of unemployment, and his dependency is increased until he is often little more than a child dressed up in adult clothes. In many cases, the alcoholic's addiction progresses to such totally unmanageable stages that his employer is forced eventually to fire him.

For the alcoholic, the tragedy of being protected by *enablers* on the job is that they interfere with the single most motivating factor for his recovery from addiction: the fear of being fired. Alcoholics who are guaranteed their jobs whether they drink or not, will drink. Those who are threatened with dismissal unless they complete treatment programs now have the highest recovery rate of any group of alcoholics. These rates begin at 60 to 70 percent and climb as high as 90 percent for our nation's airline pilots.[5]

On the job, at church, and in the doctor's office, the alcoholic encounters a wealth of community support for his addiction. It is in the family environment, however, where the alcoholic finds his greatest allies. Here, the people who suffer most from his behavior become the people who nurture his addiction. The enabling relationships which develop follow a predictable pattern and cause alcoholism to be accurately labeled "the family disease."

9

A Wife's Point of View

Linda Morgan was a loyal wife. When her husband, John, whose story was told in Chapter 7, was thrown in jail for public drunkenness, she bailed him out. When he was injured in a drunk-driving accident, she paid the hospital bills and fixed the car. She cleaned up after him when he was sick, put him to bed when he passed out, made up stories to tell his customers when he failed to show up for an auction. Although she was painfully embarrassed when John arrived drunk at his son's Little League game, she never allowed her children to complain about their father.

When John's binges began to occur with increasing frequency, Linda reluctantly asked one of her church leaders for advice. "Find out what you're doing to make him drink," the man advised. "If you treat John right, he'll settle down."

Linda stepped up her efforts to be a good wife. She fixed John's favorite foods and wore his favorite clothes. She tried never to nag him about household chores or business responsibilities, and she always covered his bad checks. When his drinking threatened his antique business, she took over the bookkeeping and helped with the sales.

At times, John went for months without drinking. Then, just as Linda began to believe his claims that he was permanently on the wagon, he would come home drunk again. While John was drinking, Linda often resolved to take the kids and leave him, but he always sobered up just before she packed her bag. After his binges, he was unusually kind and thoughtful. Despite her better judgment, Linda always felt a renewal of hope. Maybe this time John really meant it when he said he wouldn't drink again.

As John's drinking escalated, the Morgan family began to suffer genuine hardship. There were unpaid bills, cuts in the food budget, clothes that had to be worn for years. There were fights, accidents, embarrassing public scenes, and worst of all, the constant fear that John would seriously hurt himself or someone else.

Over the years, Linda began to pay a physical and emotional price for her husband's unpredictable behavior. She had headaches and high blood pressure. Sometimes she was so depressed she was unable to get out of bed in the morning. She had no emotional energy for spending time with her children, and she felt increasingly tense and angry.

"John's outlet was drinking," remembers Linda. "Mine was screaming. I became a nag—my voice grew tight and shrill, and I was always finding fault with someone or something. When I looked in the mirror at my angry, tense face, and saw the dark circles under my eyes, I blamed John for making me into an ugly, hateful person. But deep down I still believed that if only I could be a better wife, John would stop drinking."

Linda's inability to control either herself or her husband's drinking left her with a deep sense of guilt and failure. Her despair reached suicidal levels, and in desperation she began attending Al-Anon meetings.

At Al-Anon, Linda learned that she was not alone. There were millions of men and women married to alcoholics who felt and behaved just as she did. Her life had become unmanageable, but there was hope. The first step was to accept responsibility for her own actions. The second step was to let John accept responsibility for his.

"It was such a relief to hear that I didn't *cause* John's drinking, I couldn't *control* it, and I couldn't *cure* it," re-

members Linda. "But it was months before I was willing
to face my own faults. I was so used to blaming everything on John, my spiritual maturity had come to a stand-
still."

As Linda learned to surrender her life to God, she was
able to let John take responsibility for his own life. She
still remembers the night she finally gave John to the
Lord. "It was 6:30 in the evening, John was late, and I was
praying at the window. Usually I prayed with one eye
shut and one eye open, telling God what to do. This time
I told God that whatever happened I would praise him.
The burden I had been carrying for years left me right
there at the window, and I went to fix dinner for the
children."

John called late that evening. He had been arrested *at*
6:30 and now needed Linda to post bail. Linda told John
she loved him. "For the first time in years, I really meant
it," Linda says. She also told John that she would not be
coming to bail him out. She was sorry he had gotten himself into a mess, but now he would have to get himself
out.

It was the beginning of a new way of life in the Morgan
family. Linda began spending more time with the children, and they could no longer tell simply by looking at
their mother's face that their father was drinking. They
could talk with their mother about the hurt which they
had experienced, about the pain their father's drinking
and her screaming had caused them.

When John came home drunk, Linda greeted him at
the door with silence or a smile. She didn't scream, she
didn't nag, and she didn't shelter John from the consequences of his drinking. If he was sick, he cleaned himself
up. If he passed out at night on the kitchen floor, he
found himself in the same spot in the morning. When he
was in an accident, he called the tow truck, paid the damages, and made his own explanations to the children and
neighbors.

Linda also stopped doing the bookkeeping for John's
antique business. John's business associate was outraged
and warned Linda that she was leading the company into

bankruptcy. "It's a risk I'm prepared to take," Linda responded. "As long as John is drinking, I'm not helping in the business."

Now when John returned home drunk, he cried and begged Linda to become the wife he once knew. For the first time in fourteen years, Linda was unmoved by his tears. She no longer felt sorry for him. "You know where to get help," she told John. "When you're sick and tired of drinking, I know you'll go find it."

Within a year John Morgan was "sick and tired." The price of intoxication had been raised to painful levels, and he was no longer willing to live with the consequences of his addiction. With Linda's help, he entered a treatment program and began a new life without alcohol.

For Linda, John's sobriety was just one more ingredient in the slow but steady recovery of the Morgan family. In fourteen years of living with an alcoholic, none of them had escaped injury. All of them had wounds to heal, resentments to let go, wrongs to forgive. They had become sick together—as a family. Now, as a family—and by the grace of God—they were becoming well.

10

The Family Trap

Alcoholism is a family affair. It is estimated that every alcoholic deeply affects at least four people; in the United States, this means that at least forty million angry, anxious, and guilt-ridden adults and children are spending much of their life energies trying to cope with the bizarre and manipulative behavior of an alcoholic.

Outwardly, every family of an alcoholic has a different story to tell. Some live with a "quiet drunk" who so passively drinks his life away that his family suffers from nothing except his absence. Some live with a "happy drunk" whose good nature makes it difficult for family members to take his addiction seriously. Still others must cope with a violent, twisted alcoholic who terrorizes his family physically or psychologically. For these abused families, life becomes a periodic or daily nightmare unimaginable to healthy families.

Whatever personality differences exist among alcoholics, their family members frequently react in predictable ways to the strain of living with an addict. These reactions can become as obsessive and compulsive as the alcoholic's own behavior, and as such, they often threaten to leave family members clinically sicker than the alcoholic.

Family Denial

One of the most baffling aspects of alcoholism is the inability of the people closest to the alcoholic to recognize the reality of his addiction. The average family with an alcoholic member waits seven years after the evidence of addiction is indisputable to admit that there is an alcoholic in the house. They then wait another two years before seeking help. Even more puzzling, many family members and friends continue to deny the alcoholic's addiction long after he or she has died from an alcohol-related disease or accident. One recovering alcoholic writes:

> Recently a good friend of mine died of alcoholism at the age of forty-three. Doctors found her physical disabilities indicated she had been an alcoholic for a great many years. Yet six months before she died, her father told me impatiently that she wasn't an alcoholic, and named a dozen women who drank more and behaved far worse. All her friends and relations had assured her that she wasn't an alcoholic. Most of them still think she died of heart failure, a falsehood that the newspapers faithfully recorded.[1]

This persistent denial by family members and close friends, however senseless it may seem, has a peculiar logic of its own. In the early stages of addiction, there are seldom visible clues to distinguish an alcoholic from a heavy or even moderate drinker. When early warning signs do appear—increased consumption, frequent intoxication, personality change—the people closest to the alcoholic are blinded by personal loyalties and the social stigma attached to alcoholism. For all of us, it is much easier to dismiss questionable drinking behavior as perfectly normal than to entertain the possibility that someone we know well and love has developed a socially unacceptable addiction.

By the time an alcoholic is unquestionably addicted, his family and any remaining friends are caught up in the net of his sickness and often lose all ability to make an objective judgment about his condition. Several important factors contribute to the family's distorted perceptions of reality:

1. *Isolation.* It is rare to find a family that talks together about the presence of an alcoholic in their midst. Shame

and embarrassment build a wall of silence around each individual member and gradually cut off all but superficial communication. To make matters worse, the alcoholic is often remarkably skilled at playing one member of the family against another. His manipulative behavior aggravates old wounds and resentments, and effectively prevents any united opposition to his addiction.

Family members increase their isolation by gradually separating themselves from outside friends and interests. They learn from painful experience not to invite friends home, and because of the insecurities generated by the alcoholic's addiction, they have trouble forming deep relationships with people outside their family. If the children of alcoholics do have friends, it is often other children of alcoholics.

The world of the alcoholic's family members gradually narrows until it includes little more than the addicted drinker and those who circle in his orbit. This creates an increasingly comfortable drinking environment for the alcoholic and forces the family to be emotionally dependent upon him for their own sense of well-being.

2. *Emotional Turmoil.* Sooner or later, the family members of the alcoholic become trapped in much the same emotional turmoil that afflicts the alcoholic. They feel guilty for "causing" the alcoholic to drink and for hating or resenting someone they know they should love. They are ashamed and embarrassed by the alcoholic's actions. And they are angry at their own helplessness. Fear of the alcoholic's unpredictable behavior mixes with vague anxieties about the future, and increasing isolation leads to loneliness and depression.

Family members of alcoholics seldom share their emotions with others. Instead, they suppress them and allow them to fester into despair and self-hatred. Without a healthy self-image, the family is increasingly susceptible to the alcoholic's manipulation.

3. *The Centricity of the Alcoholic.* In a healthy family, no one person is always center stage. Attention is given to the needs and talents of each member, and there is a healthy give-and-take between husband and wife, parents and children.

Within his family, the alcoholic is usually the primary focus of everyone's attention. Because his behavior is unpredictable, he is "the unknown factor," and all thoughts automatically focus on him. What kind of mood is he in today? If he's sober, what will we do to keep him happy? If he's drunk, how will we pacify him? How will we stay out of his way? The family is always on guard, trying to predict the unpredictable and hoping to keep a bad situation from becoming worse.

Because the family is in emotional turmoil and becoming increasingly isolated, and because the alcoholic is the focus of their energies, family members often unconsciously adopt the alcoholic's perspective of reality. It is not that he drinks too much, but that his wife is a nag, or his children are noisy, or his parents are unfair, or his boss is a taskmaster. Family members internalize the rationalizations and projections of the alcoholic, and like the alcoholic, they can deny his addiction even while they are paying an extraordinary price for his drinking.

The Chief Enabler

Every member in the family of an alcoholic makes adjustments in his or her behavior to accommodate the alcoholic and shelter him from the consequences of his drinking. Usually, there is one person who stands out—*a chief enabler.* The chief enabler is commonly a husband or wife, but can be a child or parent, a close friend or employer, a pastor or church leader.

In the early years of addiction, the chief enabler is motivated by love and concern for the alcoholic. She senses

that he really can't control his drinking and tries to remove temptation by cutting off his supply of alcohol.*
She searches the house for hidden bottles, pours hundreds of dollars of liquor down the drain, dilutes his
drinks, and tries to engineer his social life. She is irritated
by friends who drink and "tempt" the alcoholic, and she
stops accepting invitations to parties where alcohol is
served.

Despite her efforts, the alcoholic continues to drink. In
order to survive and reduce the pressures which she be-
lieves cause her husband's addiction, the chief enabler
picks up one by one the responsibilities which the alcoholic lays down. She pays the bills, fixes the plumbing,
and disciplines the children. She also lies to his boss about
his absence from work, bails him out of jail, takes his side
in drunk driving accidents, and drives him to work when
he loses his license. Frequently, non-income-earning
wives of alcoholics must become breadwinners to replace
the income that the alcoholic drinks away.

The good intentions of the chief enabler create for the
alcoholic an increasingly comfortable environment in
which to drink. His meals are cooked, his laundry done,
his transportation provided. The alcoholic neglects the responsibilities of adulthood, and in exchange, he receives
the conveniences of life.

While the alcoholic is sheltered from the consequences
of his addiction, the chief enabler experiences more and
more failure. She cannot control her husband's drinking—or her own unpredictable emotions. She is depressed, moody, irritable, and angry. She nags and

----

*In speaking of the chief enabler, I will use the pronoun
"she" for convenience. There are, of course, many men who
enable their wives to develop and perpetuate an addiction.
Most suffer deeply from their spouses' bizarre and unpredictable behavior. A few however, encourage their wives to drink
so that they will be more relaxed and witty. Often in such cases,
even after a wife has begun to worry about her drinking, her
husband will dismiss her fears and pour her another drink.

screams when what she really wants to be is loving and kind. Her disagreeable behavior aggravates her sense of guilt and shame, and her self-esteem disappears.

The alcoholic has an uncanny ability to play on human weaknesses. He takes advantage of his wife's emotional turmoil and dependency, and zeroes in on her points of greatest vulnerability. He gives devastating critiques of her character. And just when she has had enough, he sobers up and is a genuinely charming man, the husband she thought she married. These periods of sobriety keep a wife hanging on for years, hoping that sooner or later she will find the key to solving her husband's drinking problem.

Many committed Christian women are particularly vulnerable to the emotional bondage generated by the alcoholic. They are often encouraged by church leaders to be patient and passive, to submit to their husband's authority, however abusive, and to "kill him with kindness" as part of their obedient service to God. Unfortunately, for both the alcoholic and his wife, kindness is indeed the ultimate killer. In the absence of "tough love," the alcoholic husband gets sicker, and his wife falls into a self-destructive pattern of living.

"Compassion," says the Reverend Joseph Kellerman, "is bearing with or suffering with a person, not suffering because of the unwillingness of the other person to suffer."[2] The suffering of a wife or husband of an alcoholic is seldom compassionate—or redemptive. It is a suffering poisoned by self-pity and resentment. Genuine love is replaced by a martyr complex or a secret satisfaction in the alcoholic's childlike dependence on the chief enabler. The result is often a macabre dance of sadism and masochism which threatens to destroy the image of God in both husband and wife.

Sooner or later, the chief enabler comes to the end of hope. Crying, begging, screaming, pleading, and praying have all failed. There are no more promises to be believed. In the absence of outside help, the chief enabler and other family members must now choose either to desert the alcoholic or to settle for a precarious détente.

Desertion

Some husbands, wives, parents, and children choose to leave the alcoholic. They are convinced that he is the source of all their problems, and that once he is left behind, they will be able to start a new and better life for themselves.

However, statistics show that physical separation does not heal the wounds that come from living with an alcoholic. Children of alcoholics frequently marry alcoholics or become alcoholics themselves. The wives or husbands of alcoholics may say "never again" and later marry a second alcoholic—then a third. They carry the seeds of failure with them: bitterness, resentment, guilt, low self-esteem, and anger. Sometimes, years after the alcoholic is gone, he is still the center of their fantasies for revenge and retribution.

A sad number of marriage partners and children choose to desert the alcoholic by killing themselves. In one unpublished study, two-thirds of the adolescents who successfully committed suicides had an alcoholic parent; in another study, the figure rose to 90 percent. The striking frequency of these desperate and final acts gives poignant testimony to the hopelessness which springs from living with an alcoholic.

Détente

Statistics say that while nine out of ten men leave their alcoholic wives, nine out of ten women stay with their alcoholic husbands. In happier circumstances, these figures might speak for the superior loyalty of women. Unfortunately, the reasons why women stay in alcoholic marriages are seldom healthy. Most wives of alcoholics can no more leave their husbands than their husbands can leave the bottle. They usually possess few financial resources, cannot escape their emotional dependence, and have grown accustomed to the strange mixture of control and dependency which characterizes alcoholic relationships. They are also deeply frightened by the prospect of new relationships based on mutual respect.

Wives or husbands of alcoholics who cannot or will not desert their spouses try to negotiate a détente. They do everything possible not to rock the boat, accommodating themselves and their children to the alcoholic's drinking. Most of their energies are directed at a single goal—maintaining the status quo.

Unfortunately, the alcoholic's addiction refuses to stand still. *Alcoholic détente* is a progressively unhealthy and interlocking system of relationships which impoverishes the lives of all members of the family, including the alcoholic. In this environment, the individuals most deeply hurt are the children. Caught between a sick mother and a sick father, they become the unnoticed and untreated victims of addiction.

11

"Somebody's Going to Get It!"

Mary Ruth's father was a brilliant man. His interests ranged from ancient history to scuba diving and he was a top-ranked physicist in a large chemical corporation. In addition, he had a photographic memory. Every evening he read two or three books; every day he drank a fifth of Scotch.

On the job, Mary Ruth's father was quiet and reserved. At home, he was an unpredictable tyrant who physically abused his wife and emotionally terrorized his children. He cruelly teased his sons and had an odd habit of sitting and staring at Mary Ruth while she did her homework. Sometimes he put his hand on her head and left it there. "He was like a black hole," Mary Ruth remembers. "It was as if he wanted to drain every drop of warmth from my body. Sometimes when he looked at me I ran upstairs and threw up."

Nights were always difficult. From her bedroom, Mary Ruth could hear her mother crying and her father shouting. Sometimes there was the sound of breaking furniture and glass. More than once, her father fell asleep with a burning cigarette in his hand and set fire to large areas of the living room carpet. One night he wandered into her room completely undressed and lay down on top of her. He passed out almost immediately, but Mary Ruth stayed awake until morning, trying not to move and breathing the stale smell of alcohol.

Mary Ruth never talked to anyone about her father's

drinking or strange behavior, but she did everything she could to make things easier for her mother. From an early age, she took responsibility for an unusual number of chores, including preparation of the evening meal. She protected her brothers from her father's violence and tried to comfort her mother when she was crying. At school, Mary Ruth was a model student. She worked hard to win her teacher's approval, and although she was remarkably mature and serious for her age, she was friendly and kind to all her classmates. They liked her willingness to do them favors and the attentive way she listened to everything they said.

While Mary Ruth was still in grade school, her father's drinking escalated. His liver and kidneys became seriously diseased, and he lost the use of one lung. He still reported to work every morning, but his behavior at home was increasingly sinister. The suicidal notes he left lying around the house took on a homicidal ring: "Somebody's going to get it," he threatened. Mary Ruth's mother divided the family shotgun into three parts and gave each of her children a segment to hide between his or her mattress. Like her brothers, Mary Ruth already had hidden a rope under her bed to use in case of fire. Now she became especially quick at removing knives and throwable objects from her father's reach.

One evening, when Mary Ruth was fourteen, her father fell and put his head through the television screen. After he stood up, he seemed unusually disoriented and angry. He followed Mary Ruth around as she put away the dinner dishes, staring at her with bloodshot, watery eyes. Cirrhosis had changed his skin to a strange yellow color, and his breathing was shallow and raspy. He smelled oddly sour. Mary Ruth was suddenly overwhelmed by her father's horrifying appearance and she ran upstairs to her bedroom. In her fright she had forgotten her nightly responsibility of closing the basement door. A few moments later, she heard her father crashing down the cellar steps. He fell, landing head first, and died.

Within a year of her father's death, Mary Ruth became a Christian through a nationally known high-school ministry. She attended a girl's Bible study and was a summer

staff worker at a youth ranch. Despite the intimate
friendships she found among Christian believers, she
never talked about her father or the responsibility she felt
for his death. "When you're in your teens, it's almost impossible to find someone who can relate to the pain of
growing up in an alcoholic home," says Mary Ruth. "A
normal high-school girl is worried about her fingernails
and the guy sitting next to her in class. I knew there was
no point in trying to talk about my family's experience."

Mary Ruth graduated from high school with an outstanding academic record and went to college. She immediately became a leader among Christian students on
campus and taught a Bible study in her dorm. She led
weekend retreats for high-school students, spent many
late nights counseling troubled friends, and was always
willing to type a term paper or bake brownies for late-
night study breaks. Her fellow students were attracted by
her unselfish giving and the genuine compassion with
which she helped them find solutions to their problems.
"Mary Ruth is a servant," her Christian friends said with
admiration. "She's always there when you need her."

When Mary Ruth was in her early twenties, her eye-
sight began to fail. She wore thick glasses and more than
once fainted on her way home from class. She often
threw up after her evening meal and experienced crippling attacks of anxiety. She began to stay alone in her
room, rocking back and forth, hugging her knees and
staring vacantly out the window. Sometimes she heard
voices, and twice she sweated blood through her face.
"What happened to Mary Ruth?" her friends asked in dis-
may. "She's the last person we expected to go off the deep
end!"

Mary Ruth's "deep end" lasted for two years. She went
from church to church and doctor to doctor looking for
help, until she finally found a Christian psychiatrist who
understood the unique needs of adult children of alcoholics. With his assistance, she was able to face her past
honestly and surrender her hurts to God.

"My nervous breakdown was the most painful period of
my life," recalls Mary Ruth. "But it was a gift from God.

The defense mechanisms of my childhood—compulsive giving and excessive responsibility—were remarkably strong. They had served me well for years, enabling me to withstand the stress of my father's alcoholic behavior.

"As a teenager and young adult, my defensive behavior was reinforced by my Christain experience. I spiritualized my wounds and convinced myself that compulsive giving and frenetic activity were signs of Christian maturity, part of my obedient service to God. The truth is that I grew up with a sick personality, and my relationship with Christ took the same form. Only the most painful of experiences could break through my defensive, compulsive behavior and expose it for what it really was: a crippling barrier to true spirituality and genuine love."

Today, Mary Ruth is still an unusually empathic and giving person. She has a special sensitivity to people living on the margins of society, and she is always willing to lend a hand in time of trouble. "The difference is that now I can 'let go and let God,'" explains Mary Ruth. "I don't try to control everything and fix everyone. I let people take responsibility for their own pain, and I'm no longer so eager to please or so quick to blame myself for other people's inappropriate behavior."

For Mary Ruth, the deep wounds of childhood have been transformed into gifts through which she is able to help bring genuine healing to other wounded men and women. She is one of an estimated twenty-eight million children and adult offspring of alcoholics who have grown up, or are growing up, in the shadow of an unpredictable and self-centered parent. Not all of these children have a childhood as horrifying as Mary Ruth's—some are much better, some far worse—but no child in an alcoholic home grows up undamaged. This damage can begin before birth, and almost always casts a long shadow into adulthood.

The Unborn Child

Belinda was pregnant for the first time. She was a heavy smoker and drinker, but she was very concerned

about the health of her unborn child. During her first pre-
natal checkup, her doctor explained the serious consequences of smoking during pregnancy. He did not ask
Belinda about her drinking habits. Belinda went home
and threw away her cigarettes, but she continued to
drink a half bottle or more of wine a day. In seven
months, she gave birth to a six-pound baby boy suffering
from irreversible brain damage. He was one of thousands
of babies born every year with serious alcohol-related
birth defects.

No one knows how much alcohol a pregnant woman
must drink to harm her unborn child. Alcohol crosses the
placenta freely, is rapidly absorbed into a baby's blood-
stream, and is slowly metabolized by a liver not yet fully
developed. The result is that even small amounts of alcohol (one-half ounce) can affect the breathing movements
of a child *in utero*. Moderate daily amounts of alcohol
(one ounce) have been shown to dramatically reduce a
child's birth weight.

When a childbearing woman drinks alcoholically or
heavily, there is substantial risk that her baby will be born
with *fetal alcohol syndrome*. This disturbing cluster of
serious and irreversible birth defects includes mental retardation, stunted growth, and odd facial deformities. It is
the number three cause of birth defects associated with
brain damage, and its occurrence increases every year.
No one knows how many more unborn children suffer
indirectly from maternal drinking because of falls, physical fights, and malnutrition.

The surgeon general of the United States has determined that there is *no* safe amount of alcohol which a
pregnant woman can drink. Unfortunately, a great deal of
damage can be done to an unborn child in the first seven
weeks of pregnancy, the time period when women normally are unaware that they are carrying a child. The
effects of maternal drinking are so devastating that many
legislators advocate placing warning labels for women on
alcoholic beverages. Others have recommended sending a

registered letter that warns of the consequences of drinking during pregnancy to all women between the ages of fourteen and fifty. Meanwhile, the effects of alcohol on unborn children remain a strangely well-kept secret, and the price we pay as a society for this ignorance increases every year.

The Developing Child: Too Much, Too Soon

Laura is worried. Her father drinks too much. Her mother works at a grocery store, and after school, Laura takes care of her younger brother and sisters. Her brother, age four, is already a chronic troublemaker. Her twin sisters, age five, live in a world of their own. One cries easily and hides in a closet at the first sign of trouble; the other laughs and acts silly, even when everyone else is sad. Laura tries to make her brother and sisters behave so their father won't drink, but usually they don't listen. They tell Laura she is bossy, and they refuse to do their chores.

Laura works hard to fix things for her family. She does the laundry, sweeps the floor, gives baths, and mows the lawn. When her father comes home drunk, she puts him to bed. If one of the younger children is sick, she stays home from school and babysits. She helps her mother with meals. But no matter how hard Laura works, she always feels anxious and afraid. Things are falling apart faster than she can put them together.

Laura is seven years old. She is one of an estimated fifteen million children and teenagers currently living with an alcoholic parent. (An unknown number live with two alcoholic parents.) Like most of these boys and girls, Laura is growing up too quickly in a home environment devoid of the most important ingredients of healthy childhood: love, limits, and consistency.

Few alcoholics are capable of the sustained effort necessary for communicating parental love to their children. "You showed affection only when drunk," writes one adult child to her alcoholic father. "And that kind of affection is meaningful only to another drunk person. We could be your good buddies then, and yet we hated ourselves for doing so because we knew it was just the booze talking."[1]

In many homes with an alcoholic parent, there is no talking at all. Meal times are silent affairs—or shouting matches. If children attempt to carry on a conversation with a parent, the result is often a painful monologue. "When you come home from school, and something really good or bad happened that day, you want to tell someone," says a ten-year-old child of an alcoholic. "But no one wants to listen. It's better not to get happy or sad. It's better not to feel things."

Even while the children of an alcoholic attempt to shut off their normal emotions, they are often caught up in a whirlpool of shame, embarrassment, fear, and guilt. They instinctively look up to their parent and want to admire him, but they are repelled by his alcoholic behavior. Children feel deeply responsible for their parents' drinking but are acutely aware of their own helplessness. Their welfare is tied to the whimsical fancy of a sick and unpredictable person, and no matter how hard they try, children cannot make the drinking go away.

The chronic anxiety of children of alcoholics is aggravated by the mixed signals which they receive from both parents. Discipline is often, at best, sporadic. When the alcoholic is drunk, he may be exceptionally brutal toward his children, unusually loving, or totally oblivious to their behavior. When he is sober, guilt and shame tend to cause the alcoholic to swing in the other direction. He may become extremely permissive or tyrannically strict, reversing decisions that he made while drunk. Whichever way the pendulum swings, growing children soon learn that there is only one established boundary in their lives: the mood of their alcoholic parent.

This parental inconsistency is particularly damaging to a child's moral development. Children learn the difference between right and wrong primarily in the home, and they are easily confused if parents preach one message and practice another. Frequently in alcoholic homes, both parents follow a double standard as their personal morality declines to meet the demands of addiction.

Perhaps the most common area of moral confusion for children of alcoholics rests in the difficulty they have telling the truth. Like most children, they are taught at an early age not to tell lies. Then, during their developing years, they listen to their father lie about how much he drinks, where he has been, and what he has done. They may hear their mother lying to employers, neighbors, and even the police. Often they themselves are asked to tell "white lies" to protect their parent's reputation.

This seemingly minor moral discrepancy can be a major problem for a developing child. Children of alcoholics frequently struggle with the problem of compulsive lying long after they have committed themselves to being honest adults. "For most of my life, I lied about things that didn't matter at all," says one adult child of an alcoholic. "I found myself saying preposterous things, and then I was too embarrassed to retract them. Over the years, I lost many friends because they discovered I could not be trusted.

"The turning point came when I met a man who remained my friend even after he discovered that I did not always tell the truth. His acceptance and loving confrontation enabled me to face my problem honestly. I realized that just as my father was addicted to alcohol, I was addicted to lying. Through much prayer and hard work, I learned as an adult what most people learn as children—how to tell the truth."

The moral unpredictability of the alcoholic can extend even further to physical abuse. Each year in the United States alone, fifty thousand children are seriously injured by their parents and two thousand are killed. It is believed that drinking parents account for nearly 80 percent of these cases of child abuse and that over half of all alcoholic parents physically abuse their children on a regular basis. These statistics, however heartrending, cannot adequately communicate the terror of a defenseless child who, year after year, is physically and psychologically tortured by a violent and unpredictable parent. For many of these children, survival becomes a full time job, and their nightmare ends only when they are driven to suicide or murder.

The Paralysis of the Non-Drinking Parent

Whatever level of abuse or neglect comes to exist in an alcoholic home, when problems first begin to develop, young children automatically turn to their non-drinking parent for emotional and spiritual support. Only a few find it. In some families, the non-drinking parent is able to put aside his or her own pain and focus attention on the critical needs of a child growing up in a crisis-oriented environment. More commonly, however, the wife or husband of an alcoholic is too exhausted by the day-to-day trauma of living with an addicted spouse to give even normal amounts of attention to children, much less the extra parenting which is needed. The love they mean to demonstrate comes wrapped in a garment of fatigue and chronic irritation. Their preoccupation and frustration signal to the child that he or she is unloved and unwanted, and instead of becoming allies in a difficult situation, children and parents become increasingly burdensome to one another.

Frequently, children of alcoholics feel angrier at their non-drinking parent than at the alcoholic. They may sympathize with the alcoholic as a weak or sick person, but they see their non-drinking mother or father as a powerful adult who could put a stop to the family's problems if he or she tried. The child is further alienated from the non-alcoholic parent by the rationalizations and accusations of the alcoholic, which become increasingly believable as the behavior of the non-alcoholic parent becomes more and more erratic. The child may come to blame the non-alcoholic parent for all the family's problems, including the alcoholic's drinking.

A child's feelings of helpless anger toward the non-alcoholic parent are intensified in homes where children are physically abused. In *Murphy's Boy,* child psychologist

Torey Hayden tells the story of a young boy who is abused by his alcoholic stepfather. The boy develops a pathological hatred for his mother, who remains a passive spectator to her husband's abuse and refuses to interfere when her seven-year-old daughter is beaten to death. Her son says:

> I was crying and screaming at him, but my mom she just stood there. And I yell at her, I say to my mom, "*Help* her! Make him *stop!*" And my mom just stood there. She says, "Leave them alone. It isn't any of your business. . . . "
> You know what. I seen [my sister's] brains come out. . . . And my mom seen. My momma seen the whole thing. . . . And she never once did a thing."[2]

For this crime, the boy's stepfather spent four years in jail. Upon his release, he returned to his family and continued to abuse his stepson until the boy was hospitalized with critical injuries. At this point, the state intervened and took the boy from his parents, but he had already suffered profound physical and psychological damage.

A Crisis of Confidence

With one parent unpredictable and the other emotionally paralyzed, the children of an alcoholic quickly learn that they cannot depend on their parents to meet their basic needs. This is a devastating vacuum in the life of a dependent child. Children learn the art of trusting others by first trusting their parents. If they are forced to surrender their natural dependence prematurely, they become deeply suspicious and mistrustful of their fellow human beings. While a certain amount of skepticism is necessary and prudent, the inability to establish relationships based on mutual trust is a paralyzing emotional handicap. It is a legacy which effectively isolates children of alcoholics from the deep friendships and commitments necessary for healthy personality development.

Children who cannot rely on their parents are forced to rely on themselves. Unfortunately for children of alcoholics, their external and internal resources are substantially more limited than those of even ordinary children. They have bad role models for handling stress and crises, and little experience with spontaneous, flexible behavior. They are left to guess which parental behaviors are considered normal human responses. Usually they have no one with whom they can talk over their confusion. This confusion is then aggravated by the whirl of their strong, unexpressed, and usually twisted emotions.

Worst of all, the child of an alcoholic often suffers from a critical deficiency in his or her self-respect. Self-esteem is not an instinct; children must learn to value themselves by experiencing loving approval and consistent discipline from their parents. What children of alcoholics experience is constant criticism. They always fall short of the perfectionism and unrealistic expectations of their addicted parent, and their fledgling sense of self-confidence is undercut by a paralyzing sense of inadequacy. "I could never do enough to please my father," says one adult child of an alcoholic. "He was so demanding that we were forced to sweep all the stones in our driveway in the same direction. I grew up with a tremendous fear of not producing, of being caught doing nothing."

Crippled by insecurity and still in the tender stages of personality development, children of alcoholics are often asked to handle increasingly difficult circumstances. The methods they use to survive—and children of alcoholics are survivors—reveal a great deal about the human personality and its sophisticated techniques for coping with crises.

12

Games Children Play

Children grow up by trial and error. They try out a variety of ways of responding to an unfamiliar world and eventually discover what works and what does not. They learn when it is best to take charge, when to give in, when to think for themselves, and when to respect the opinions and needs of others. They make frequent miscalculations, but gradually they adjust their behavior to fit the changing nature of their environment and relationships.

For most children of alcoholics, this flexible maturation process is an unaffordable luxury. In order to cope with an unpredictable parent, they often lock themselves into rigid roles within the family system very early in life. While it may outwardly appear normal and healthy, this defensive behavior can be as compulsive and obsessive as the alcoholic's addiction.

The coping styles or family roles of children of alcoholics include: (a) becoming unusually responsible; (b) being a compulsive servant or "placater"; (c) always adjusting or giving in; and (d) causing trouble.[1] Whether a child adopts one role or a combination of roles, his defensive behavior usually serves him well for years. It compensates for parental inadequacies, covers the gaps in his emotional development, and brings a semblance of stability and order to an otherwise chaotic life. Because they have learned to trust its reliability, children carry their coping strategy into adulthood where, under the strain of adult relationships and responsibilities, they come face-to-face with the dark side of their developmental years.

The Responsible Child: A Family Hero

In almost every disrupted family there is usually one child, often the oldest, who takes on the duties of a missing or overburdened parent. This responsible, adult-like child prepares meals, worries about finances, looks out for the welfare of younger brothers and sisters, and tries to keep the family functioning as normally as possible. Sometimes the child plays the role of counselor, settling disputes between his parents and trying to smooth over broken relationships. Sometimes he plays the role of "enabler," bringing the alcoholic parent home from bars, cleaning up after him when he is sick, and pouring out his liquor supply. One teenage boy, in order to prevent his alcoholic mother from falling down the stairs at night, regularly slept on the floor in front of her bedroom door.

At school, the *family hero* is usually an overachiever. He may make above-average grades, run for class office, or be a disciplined athlete. He works hard to accomplish difficult goals and win the approval of teachers and authority figures. Often he is a gifted organizer or unusually adept at leading his classmates.

As overachieving children become adults, they commonly cover the gaps in their emotional development with hard work and self-discipline. Their inner drive to achieve leads them into early professional success and to positions of leadership within their churches and communities. They are admired for "making good" in spite of a bad home life.

While outwardly these hard-working men and women appear self-confident and capable, inwardly they are still victimized by childhood wounds. One adult child of an alcoholic, a minister, poignantly describes the emotional turmoil in which he spent much of his ministry: "I was always extremely tense. I had an inner drive to please people and the feeling that I never quite did. I dismissed compliments almost before I heard them, knowing that they surely sprang from misperceptions. I knew I had a gift for motivating and leading people, but I panicked if I wasn't in charge. Either I was calling the shots, or I felt like my whole world was crumbling."

The need to be in control makes the adult who had been an overly responsible child uncomfortable in relationships without an established hierarchy. He avoids adult friendships (and the unpredictability which they entail), and surrounds himself with people who can be controlled and manipulated. His rigid, black-and-white approach to problems alienates him from other healthy adults, and he feels increasingly lonely and depressed.

Despite emotional isolation, the family hero continues to accept more and more challenging responsibilities. He finds himself surrounded by people and circumstances he can't control, and his anxiety escalates. As a child, he learned to handle stress by working harder; now as an adult he is ignorant of the art of relaxation or letting go. He does not know how to play or take time for fun, and he cannot share his anxieties with anyone. All he can do is try harder to control himself and other people. His behavior becomes increasingly rigid and defensive, and he takes on bigger and more demanding projects. The greater his responsibilities, the more insecure he feels; and the more insecure he feels, the more responsibility he accepts. In this manner, the family hero may spend years compulsively feeding the very fire he is trying to extinguish.

The Placater-Servant

The placating child lives her life in the orbit of other people's feelings. As a young child, she is unusually sensitive to the hurts and needs of her family members, and she tries hard to diminish their disappointments and fears. She is quick to pick up on signals—of anger, hurt, resentment, sadness. She tries to smooth over conflicts before they develop and attempts to heal the hurts of others by giving of herself.

As the *placater-servant* enters adulthood, she is often surrounded by a host of so-called friends who are attracted to her unselfish giving and compassion. She is an empathic counselor, a listening person who seldom disagrees with anyone. She may apologize endlessly for events outside of her control: "I'm sorry your dinner burned. . . . I'm sorry you don't feel well. . . . I'm sorry your boss is unfair." The placating child accepts responsibilities that others avoid and, no matter how busy she becomes, she seldom says no to requests for her help.

The compulsive giving of the placater cuts her off from the mutual give-and-take of adult relationships. She is convinced that the high regard of her friends depends on her ability to outgive other people, and she is unable to receive love and concern for herself. She becomes increasingly lonely and depressed, but she cannot share her feelings with anyone; all her relationships are built on the myth of her own indestructability and lack of emotional needs.

In some disrupted families, the placating child is also the family clown. These unusually perceptive children have a knack for turning even the most awkward moments into a joke and they learn to diffuse anger or violence with well-placed humor. As they enter adulthood, family clowns frequently become compulsive talkers and are unusually high strung. Even in the most painful moments, they cover their deepest feelings with a joke. Only the most persistent and perceptive of friends can break through their cover of humor to dress the wounds that lie beneath.

The Adjuster

In the unpredictable environment of an alcoholic home, anything can happen. The *adjusting child* is always prepared—to do nothing. He is an adapter, a child so paralyzed by his own inadequacies that he no longer tries to initiate actions of his own. Instead, he opts for a relatively pain-free existence of "going with the flow." Accepting with a shrug the arbitrarily canceled vacation, the sudden fight, the unexpected slap, he recognizes that the only unchanging conditions of his life are his powerlessness and isolation. He often separates himself from his family and spends an inordinate time alone in his room, creating a fantasy world.

At school and at church, the adjuster is a "lost child," the youngster whose name no one remembers, the boy or girl whose shy and apathetic presence seldom leaves more than a fleeting impression. In a room full of noisy children clamoring for attention, the adjusting child easily slips between the cracks—and is happy there. He or she prefers to be left alone, having learned that daydreams are safer and more satisfying than unpredictable human encounters.

As the adjuster enters adulthood, he seldom has a sense of life's direction and purpose. He continues to perceive himself as powerless, a person without choices or alternatives. He usually gravitates toward people who are as emotionally detached as himself or marries a spouse who recreates the chaos of his childhood. In such marriages, the adjusting adult-child does what he knows best—he adapts. He becomes a passive spectator to the family's difficulties and is easily manipulated by people around him.

The emotional detachment and apathy of the adjusting child is often mistaken for serenity. Serenity comes when we accept the things we cannot change, but the adjusting child, sadly, accepts the fact that he cannot change anything—ever. As the years go by, this acceptance leads him farther and farther from the peace and tranquility he seeks. He becomes trapped in loneliness and despair.

The Rebellious Child

In most disrupted families, there is at least one child whose name spells T-R-O-U-B-L-E. For this child, the rules are made to be broken. He thumbs his nose at authority—

at home, at school, at church, and downtown. He is so constantly in trouble that he soon becomes the family scapegoat. Drawing attention away from the alcoholic, he is often singled out as the source of the family's growing number of problems.

The rebellious child has discovered an important principle of child development: Negative attention is better than no attention at all. His self-esteem, if it exists, is even lower than that of his performance-oriented siblings. He roots his fragile sense of self in the awareness that he is "bad," and he gravitates toward friends who likewise have poor self-esteem. Often he runs with a "wild crowd" of children or teenagers who instinctively head for trouble wherever it can be found.

Because drugs and alcohol are a common focus of teenage rebellion, the troubled child of an alcoholic is likely to experiment with or abuse addictive substances at an early age. The possibility of an inherited predisposition for addiction increases the likelihood that he will be in serious trouble with drugs or alcohol, or both, before he has left adolescence. And regardless of whether or not he develops a full-fledged addiction, the rebellious child is at high risk for spending at least part of his adolescence in reform school or a mental institution.

The rebellious child enters adulthood with a chip on his shoulder and an instinct for making poor decisions. He drops out of school, marries early or has illegitimate children, avoids job training, and runs up unpayable debts. His ability to survive in the adult world by legal means is seriously hampered by the shortsighted decisions of his youth, and he feels increasingly powerless and insignificant. His growing frustration propels him in the direction of violent and illegal acts.

When Coping Strategies Fail

Whether or not a child of an alcoholic becomes responsible, placating, adjusting, or rebellious, or tries out a combination of these roles, sooner or later his coping strategy breaks down. The behavior which was a blessing for him as a child becomes a burden to him as an adult, and he experiences unexpected failures. He discovers that not everyone can be manipulated, and those who can be eventually react with anger and bitterness. He encounters people who will not be placated and situations to which he cannot adjust. Lies catch up with the compulsive liar and even the rebellious adult child finds that the price of adult delinquent behavior has been raised beyond that which he is willing to pay.

The breakdown of old roles and behavior patterns may take decades, but when it happens, adult children of alcoholics feel suddenly bereft. The gaps in their emotional development are exposed, and old insecurities demand their due. At this point, the child often enters a new period of crises which may threaten his or her career, marriage, sanity—or life.

The Adult Crisis

Anne Murphy was an intelligent, well-dressed, and serious woman. She was also the mother of four grown children, a high-school teacher, and the wife of a likeable, easy-going Presbyterian minister. She worked hard, and while sometimes she resented her husband's lightheartedness and her own role as the family "heavy," she had been happily married for thirty years. She enjoyed teaching, and she willingly helped her husband in his church work.

One Christmas, when the family was together for the holidays, Anne's children uncorked an expensive bottle of wine. Anne was not a drinker—her childhood had been made miserable by an alcoholic father—but now with her own children grown, she felt more tolerant. She accepted a glass of wine, and then a second. She was surprised how good two drinks made her feel. She became relaxed and carefree, and for the first time in her married life, she understood her husband's jokes.

During the same holiday, over another bottle of wine, Anne and her oldest daughter had a long and intimate conversation. It had always been difficult for Anne to talk freely about her feelings. Now, with a drink in hand, she spoke candidly about her doubts and insecurities. Her daughter was sympathetic—and grateful. "I felt like I never knew you before," she said, giving her mother a rare hug. "It's like discovering a new and wonderful member of the family."

In the months that followed, Anne found that a glass of wine was a reliable method for relieving the pressures of a lifetime of difficult responsibilities. While drinking, she no longer felt as if she were missing some key to life which everyone else automatically possessed. Instead, she was learning to be in control. Her friends and family responded warmly to "the new Anne," and it seemed to Anne that a heavy burden of isolation and anxiety had suddenly dropped from her shoulders.

In three years, Anne had a new burden. She was an alcoholic. To her own horror, she was drinking up to a bottle of wine a day. She made frequent resolutions to quit, but it seemed impossible to pass up a drink at dinner. Somehow one drink always led to another, and Anne spent her evenings sprawled in front of the television, too drunk to talk coherently. In the mornings, she woke up with a headache, hating herself and counting the hours until dinner time.

Like Anne, almost all children of alcoholics grow up declaring, "It will never happen to me." They have seen firsthand the misery of addiction, and they are convinced that these grim experiences are adequate protection against marrying an alcoholic or becoming alcoholics themselves. They leave home thinking that their problems are behind them, and, in comparison to the misery of their past, their future seems remarkably bright.

Unfortunately, adult children of alcoholics carry their past with them like a time bomb waiting to explode. Although many leave home as early as possible to escape the alcoholic, 30 percent of the children of alcoholics marry alcoholics, and 50 percent of them become alcoholics. Many, like Anne, are unsuspecting adults who late in life discover that alcohol serves as a quick chemical solution to the unresolved conflicts of their childhood. With a drink, the family hero can relax, the placater can forget about other people's feelings, the adjuster feels a new sense of power and self-confidence. Unaware that inheritance patterns place them at high risk for developing addiction, these men and women quickly move from social drinking to compulsive drinking. Before they or their families know what is happening, they develop an addiction to the chemical they have feared and hated all their lives.

Addiction and alcoholic marriages are only two of the threats facing adult children of alcoholics. Often in their twenties or early thirties, they discover that their childhood defense mechanisms are falling apart under the combined pressures of marriage, children, and professional responsibilities. With no personal resources to fall back on, these men and women are often forced to extreme and desperate acts. A young minister with three children collapses in the pulpit and later takes his own life; a well-known youth worker in a major metropolitan city, a gifted young woman whom hundreds of teenagers look to for spiritual leadership, becomes suddenly depressed and is institutionalized with a psychotic breakdown; an elder in a tightly knit house church runs off with a girl half his age, leaving his wife and children in a financial and spiritual crisis.

The truth is that the passage of time seldom heals the wounds of children of alcoholics. Unless they get help for their deep psychological and spiritual difficulties, *for the remainder of their lives they will be at high risk* for the development of addiction or emotional collapse. And chances are they will pass these problems on to their children and grandchildren, who will become just one more link in a chain of alcoholic damage which stretches from generation to generation.

Fortunately, help is available. There is an effective program of recovery for the alcoholic—and his family.

13

Five Myths of Addiction

The three leading causes of death in the United States are heart disease, cancer, and alcoholism. Among these three, alcoholism occupies a unique position: It is completely *preventable;* and it is highly *treatable.* Almost without exception, any alcoholic who gets appropriate help and is willing to participate in his or her own recovery can lead a sober, productive life.

At the same time, alcoholism is one of the *least* treated of all treatable chronic disorders: Nine out of ten alcoholics never even try to get help for their addiction. Family members, close friends, and employers almost always share in this paralysis, and no matter how high the price of addiction becomes, they remain passive spectators of the alcoholic's self-destruction.

As we begin our examination of the recovery process, it is important that we appreciate the numerous obstacles which stand between an alcoholic and the help he needs. Some of these barriers have been discussed in previous chapters—the alcoholic's denial, the well-meaning but ineffective efforts of family and friends, the social stigma attached to addiction, and the frequently misleading advice of professional helpers, such as doctors, pastors, and psychologists. Moreover, the alcoholic is almost always the master in one-to-one counseling situations, and traditional methods of therapy usually only feed the alcoholic's delusion. At the same time, families who seek outside help are seldom informed of the existence of successful recovery programs. Instead, they are discouraged by experiences with second-rate treatment centers or organizations which take a simplistic approach to addiction. Their hopes have been raised and dashed one too many times. Finally, they find giving up and accepting the alcoholic for what he is easier than risking another disappointment.

To add to these formidable problems, there are many widely held myths of addiction that discourage people close to an alcoholic from interfering with the course of his alcoholism. These myths include:

1. *The alcoholic must want help before he can get it.* "Every night I begged God to help me," remembers one recovering alcoholic. "I asked him to get me out of trouble, to make me feel better, not to let me die, and to help me get around all the things that stood between me and my next drink. The only thing I never asked him was to help me stop drinking."

It is the rare alcoholic who wants help to quit drinking. Despite periods of desperation and perhaps frequent emotional appeals for assistance, the alcoholic's primary concern is to protect his liquor supply. Many recovering alcoholics testify that even when circumstances compelled them into treatment centers or Alcoholics Anonymous, they went hoping to find a way to drink without paying the steep price of addiction. They claim if they had known in advance that recovery required total abstinence, they would have stayed home.

Many alcoholics eventually find themselves echoing the desperate prayer said by one alcoholic housewife: "Lord, I need help. I don't want help, but I need help." Meanwhile, family members and friends must realize that if they patiently wait for the alcoholic to manifest a sincere desire to quit drinking, his addiction will progress to more serious and untreatable stages. The longer he drinks, the stronger his craving for alcohol becomes, and the less likely it is that he will ever ask for assistance.

2. *The alcoholic must hit rock bottom before he can get help.* An extraordinary number of family members and friends, because they have heard that alcoholics must hit

bottom before they can be rescued, stand by, helplessly watching while someone they love drinks alcoholically. This theory was popularized by early groups of Alcoholics Anonymous and was rooted in their experience that only the most desperate and hopeless of circumstances could compel an alcoholic to choose sobriety over alcohol.

It is true that an alcoholic must be allowed to experience the painful consequences of his addiction before he will give up alcohol. But it is also true that alcoholics take their first step toward recovery because they fear the loss of something or someone they value. At rock bottom, most alcoholics have nothing to lose—except a bottle. Alcohol is their single comfort in life, and with no earthly incentive for becoming sober, they steadily drink themselves to a bottom from which they cannot return: death, insanity, or institutionalization.

Today we know that, statistically speaking, the farther the alcoholic is from "the bottom," the more likely it is that he or she will achieve sobriety. A drinker who has a family, a job, physical health, friends, and mental clarity has an outstanding chance of recovering from addiction. When his addiction progresses to the point where he loses one or more of these dimensions of life, his prospects for recovery drop accordingly. If, finally, he is sleeping under a bridge, eating food from a can, and talking to himself, then there is almost no possibility that he will recover.*

3. *The alcoholic will quit drinking on his own.* Almost every family of an alcoholic waits expectantly for the day when the alcoholic will spontaneously stop drinking. They have heard stories of other alcoholics who "just up and quit," and they believe that sooner or later the alcoholic in their family will come to his senses. Their hopes are fueled by the alcoholic's ability to sober up for weeks

---

* There are notable exceptions to this rule (almost everyone has heard of a businessman, politician, doctor or lawyer who has recovered from a skid-row existence), and it is wrong to rule out hope for any human being. At the same time, the drama of these stories lies in the fact that such recoveries are the exception, not the rule.

or months at a time and occasionally exhibit charming behavior. This duality in his personality convinces family and friends that the alcoholic *could* stop drinking, if only he *would,* and that someday he will choose to sober up.

It is true that a small percentage of alcoholics spontaneously quit drinking at some time in their lives, often as part of the aging process. However, *nine out of every ten alcoholics* will drink themselves to death unless something or someone interferes with their addiction. With only the smallest possibility of a spontaneous remission, there is no medical or moral justification for watching and waiting while an alcoholic drinks.

4. *The alcoholic has a right to drink; no one has a right to interfere.* "Joe's in rough shape, but if he wants to drink, that's his choice. It's none of our business." The concepts of personal liberty and freedom of choice have little, if any, application to people addicted to chemical substances. While many decisions are involved in the development of an addiction, addiction itself marks the end of free choice. "People choose to be social drinkers," said one recovering alcoholic. "No one chooses to become an alcoholic."

To become an alcoholic is to lose one's ability not to drink. To interfere with the natural course of this addiction is no more an infringement on personal liberty than throwing a life preserver to a drowning swimmer. The swimmer may refuse the lifeline, but the offer itself is an attempt to restore freedom, not take it away. And as appropriate as it is to assist an alcoholic or a drug addict after an overdose, it is far more helpful to interrupt the addiction before it has destroyed the drinker and his family.

5. *Efforts to help the alcoholic might make his drinking worse.* People who live within the orbit of an alcoholic almost always have a paralyzing fear of upsetting the status quo, however unpleasant it may be. Despite the alcoholic's unpredictability, those around him learn to create for themselves islands of stability and order. The peace they find is often as fragile as the relief they feel when the

alcoholic drinks himself into a stupor and can be put to bed. Nonetheless, it is still a comfort. The prospect of interfering with the alcoholic's addiction or making changes in the family's hard-earned routine only raises the frightening specter of a return to chaos.

The alcoholic plays on these fears with remarkable skill. At the first sign of potential interference with his drinking, his powers of manipulation increase tenfold. Sometimes he attempts to solicit sympathy or imply that he is being "stabbed in the back," betrayed by the very people he trusts the most. Sometimes he threatens to double his drinking or physically harm himself or his family. Occasionally he threatens to leave home permanently. (This threat, while unusually effective with family members, is almost always empty. The alcoholic will not abandon a loyal group of enablers without knowing where he can find another.) Whatever tactics the alcoholic uses, his message is always the same: There is a price to pay for rocking the boat.

The truth is that, while the alcoholic and his enablers live in fear of change, there is no standing still with an addiction. Medically speaking, alcoholism is a *progressive* disease. If left to run its course, it gets worse, not better. At any given time, the alcoholic may appear to be holding his own, or even recovering, but the overall direction of his life remains the same—downhill. Driven by an overwhelming craving and blinded by denial, he slides into spiritual, psychological, physical, and social destruction. Each aspect of his sickness reinforces the others, and he is trapped in a cage which seldom opens from the inside.

Friends and family members suffer from the same devastating progression. The longer the alcoholic drinks, the more adept he becomes at manipulation, and the less able his enablers are to resist his efforts. Instead, they are caught in a self-perpetuating circle of resentment, anger, fear, guilt, and poor self-esteem. Their twisted emotions increase their dependency on the alcoholic, and they become even more vulnerable to his manipulative behavior.

This destructive downward spiral of drinking, manipulation, and enabling will not stop itself. It must be interrupted. The system of relationships that supports the alcoholic's addiction must be broken up, and the same family members, friends, and employers who shelter the alcoholic must be equipped with tools to confront him with the consequences of his addiction.

14

Steps of Preparation

The middle-aged man sitting across from my desk was deeply disturbed. He and his two grown daughters had come to see me about his wife's drinking problem, but after listening to me outline a program of recovery, he was convinced that I had not understood the seriousness of his wife's condition. "You don't know Sarah," he said emphatically. "Her case is different. Sometimes I think she's just plain crazy. She blames everything on me, and if I even mention the word *alcoholic,* she flies into a rage. Whatever you have in mind, I can tell you, 'It won't work.'"

Sarah's daughters confirmed the hopelessness of their mother's condition. Sarah spent her days swinging back and forth between depression and hysteria. There were only a few moments each morning when she was rational enough to carry on a conversation. She was extremely sensitive, and although she used Valium to settle her nerves, she was prone to violent rages. During these episodes, she verbally and physically abused her family and made shocking accusations against her husband. Everyone in the family worked hard at not upsetting Sarah, and after fifteen years of watching her drink alcoholically, they knew better than to interfere with her drinking. "We appreciate your concern," the eldest daughter concluded. "But there is no way our mother will ever admit she is an alcoholic, much less accept outside help."

Like Sarah's husband and daughters, almost every family member, friend, or employer of an alcoholic who comes through my office has at least a dozen good reasons why a program of recovery won't work in their particular circumstances. They know all too well the alcoholic's stubborn commitment to drinking. They are intimidated by his erratic behavior and painfully aware that the alcoholic has the upper hand in all his relationships. Their home remedies have failed, they believe they have exhausted their influence with the alcoholic, and they are convinced that he has been drinking for too many years to get help. However encouraging I may try to be, the problem remains as real as the drunken disorder of their home, but the solution seems as remote and ineffective as a fairy tale. Maybe it works for other people, but it will never work for them.

In Sarah's case, her husband and daughters were desperate enough to try anything. They remained pessimistic about the outcome of their efforts, but they agreed to follow the first steps of the program of recovery and prepare themselves for a group confrontation with Sarah. ("She's too tough," her husband said. "She'll never stand for it.") The confrontation took place within a month, and twenty-four hours later, to her family's astonishment, Sarah packed her bags and headed for an alcoholism treatment center. During her first week of treatment, she called home eight times, demanding that her husband immediately come rescue her from "drunks and low-lifes." At the beginning of the second week, she sent for her bathrobe and makeup. In the closing days of treatment, she admitted she was powerless over alcohol and asked God to help her stay sober "one day at a time." The road ahead included many difficulties, but today Sarah, the "hopeless" alcoholic, has been sober for nine years.

The good news about the program of recovery for addiction is this: It works. Furthermore, it doesn't depend for its success on the hopefulness or confidence of family members and friends. Even in the presence of crippling insecurities, almost anyone who is willing to follow step-by-step directions can be equipped with effective tools for confronting the alcoholic with his addiction and breaking free from the family disease of alcoholism. This effort is not without difficulties, but it takes far less energy to attempt to rescue an alcoholic than to live with one year after year. And the potential reward is as great as the redemption of the alcoholic and the healing of all those who suffer from his behavior.

As we begin this how-to portion of our investigation, a word of caution is in order. Confrontation with an alcoholic is not a one-time event; it is a *process*. This process is made up of individual steps whose order as it appears in the following pages is not accidental. Tasks required at one stage presuppose information or insights gained from prior stages, and no step should be omitted or undertaken out of its sequential order.

It is also important to remember that there is no secondhand process of preparation. *Reading* is not the same as *doing,* and an actual confrontation with the alcoholic should never be attempted without active, personal participation in all the preliminary steps. As more than one person has learned from bitter experience, a hasty and ill-formed effort will almost always end in disaster and may ruin future efforts to help the alcoholic.

STEP 1: Intercessory Prayer

Alcoholism and drug addiction are among the most profoundly spiritual of all the problems I deal with as a physician. While reducing addiction to its spiritual dimension is one-sided and ineffective, ignoring or underestimating the spiritual is equally dangerous. All those who attempt to help an alcoholic overcome addiction soon discover that they are involved in one of the most intense forms of spiritual warfare known to man.

For this reason, the first step in the program of recovery is to acknowledge our dependence on God and through prayer give ourselves and the alcoholic to his care. To take this step, it is not necessary to be a "prayer giant." Many people are so spiritually drained by years of living with an alcoholic that the only prayer they can manage is: "Oh, God, if you are there, help me!" Others, through years of spiritual discipline, are deeply aware of the presence of God's Holy Spirit and can intercede for the alcoholic with fervent, faithful prayers. Whatever our manner of talking to God may be, we must rest assured that he hears the cries of his children.

The prayers of surrender and intercession of which I am speaking are not afterthoughts or hopeless last measures to be applied when scientific efforts have failed. Rather, they are the cornerstone of all our actions under heaven and a sign of our willingness to allow God's Spirit to invade our lives. In my medical practice, I consider prayer to be the most important therapy at my disposal, and I would no more be without my ability to pray for and with my patients than I would be without my stethoscope. Prayer and science, I have learned, are noncompetitive vessels of God's grace. It is not that one starts up where the other leaves off, but that both together are agents of divine healing.

STEP 2: Education

Not long ago, I was invited to speak to an association of church ministers about alcoholism and the importance of establishing educational programs on this subject within the church. During the question and answer period which followed, one man stood up and quietly related to the group a disturbing event from the ministry of a fellow pastor:

> Several years earlier, a member of the pastor's congregation was admitted to an alcoholism treatment center at a local hospital. The pastor was skeptical about the whole concept of "treatment," and shortly after the man's admission, the pastor paid him a visit. Signs were posted forbidding visitors during the first ten days, but the pastor was sure they didn't apply to him.
>
> The pastor met with his parishioner in his room and immediately began lecturing him about his relationship to God and

his responsibility to his family. A nurse overheard the pastor's conversation and tried to persuade him to leave. Eventually, she succeeded.

As the pastor was taking the elevator to his car, his alcoholic parishioner complained that he was thirsty and sent his nurse out for a glass of water. When she returned with the drink, his window was broken, and he was lying dead by the door of the pastor's car—seven stories below his room. I wish my pastor friend had known then what I've learned today about addiction.

It is impossible to overemphasize the importance of education for people participating in a program of recovery for the alcoholic. An enormous amount of damage is done by well-intentioned but misinformed *helpers,* and the tragedy is that most of these mistakes could be prevented by a minimal amount of directed study. Nine hours of reading and viewing films is all the time it takes for anyone to inform him or herself of the essential facts about addiction. (A list of outstanding books, films, and education resources is available in Appendix C at the back of this book.) With this modest educational effort, the minister who was mentioned above would have known an important truth: Almost all alcoholics privately suffer from remorse and despair, and the quickest way to kill an addicted drinker is to exacerbate his pronounced sense of guilt without offering him a specific, effective *plan of recovery.*

For family members in particular, education plays a critical role in the recovery process. When wives, husbands, children, and parents recognize themselves and the alcoholic on film and in books, their reaction is almost always enormous relief. For the first time, they understand that they are not alone in their strange dilemma. The irrational behavior which has terrified them for years is part of a universal and diagnosable pattern of addiction. When family members realize that this pattern is not unbreakable, their relief turns to cautious hope—alcoholics as seemingly untreatable and unreachable as the alcoholics in their own lives have permanently given up drinking.

As family members learn the hard facts of addiction,

they acquire the emotional detachment necessary to overcome their fear and their dependency on the alcoholic. Eventually, family members will need to deal in depth with their own damaged emotions, but at this point in the recovery process they desperately require the perspective and healing distance which education gives. It is this objectivity which allows them to think and behave rationally enough to implement the remaining steps of the recovery program.

The data which family members acquire in the process of education are essential tools for confrontation with the alcoholic. "Frothy emotional appeal seldom suffices," said the physician whose pioneering efforts inspired the founding fathers of Alcoholics Anonymous. "The message which can interest and hold these people must have depth and weight."[1] In my own experience, the effectiveness of family members in the confrontation process is directly related to the seriousness with which they have approached their need for education.

STEP 3: Find a Support Group

Linda Morgan, whose story we read in Chapter 9, clearly remembers her first visit to an Al-Anon family group. "By then my husband had been drinking alcoholically for thirteen years," she recalls. "But the reason I went to Al-Anon was to find out how I could keep him from becoming *one of them.* Before the meeting, I checked out all the cars in the parking lot to make sure there was no one there I knew. Then I turned up the collar of my coat and snuck in the back door. If I had been going to a house of prostitution, I couldn't have felt worse.

"The minute I walked into the room I knew I was in the wrong place. Everyone was laughing and joking, and they didn't have bags under their eyes or haggard faces. They were so well-dressed and confident that I was sure none of them had ever lived with a heavy drinker."

Although Linda was unimpressed with her first meeting, she continued to attend Al-Anon because of the persistence of one of its members. She resented the smoking and occasional rough language, but every week she found something that gave her a new sense of courage and self-worth. She was amazed to find that other people felt exactly the way she did, and she was able to talk about her bitterness and chronic feelings of guilt.

"They didn't act like it was my fault that John drank," remembers Linda. "And they didn't make me feel stupid or incompetent because I couldn't handle it. From week to week, I gained confidence in myself, and then one day I discovered that I no longer hated my husband. I saw him as a sick man who didn't want to be the way he was, and I knew that with God's help and loving support from friends in Al-Anon, I would find the strength and serenity to let my husband experience the consequences of his addiction."

Al-Anon is an extraordinary, worldwide fellowship for the family and friends of alcoholics. There are over twenty thousand Al-Anon groups around the world, including twenty-five hundred Alateen groups for adolescents. Members meet weekly to "help themselves and others overcome the frustration and helplessness caused by living or having lived with an alcoholic."[2] This help comes from the time-tested process of identifying with one another's struggles and following a group of spiritual principles commonly known as "The Twelve Steps." (These principles, which are likewise essential to the recovery of the alcoholic, are discussed in detail in Chapter 18.) As with any self-help movement, some Al-Anon groups are more effective than others, but family members and friends who regularly attend meetings find a wealth of moral support and practical help for their own efforts to recover from the family disease of addiction. Literature available at Al-Anon helps further the education of would-be helpers. Some is designed to be left around the house for the alcoholic's attention.

Over the years, I have observed that participation in Al-Anon is an essential step in the recovery process. While some people may be discouraged by thick smoke, rough language, and the mysteries of group jargon, none of these hurdles is insurmountable. I recommend to all my patients that they attend at least six meetings before they decide that Al-Anon is not for them. By that time most of them find that the benefits of these meetings far outweigh any difficulties they may encounter.

Most communities have one or more existing Al-Anon groups whose phone numbers are available in the local telephone directory. For people living in remote areas or in locations where there are not yet Al-Anon groups, further information and assistance can be obtained by writing Al-Anon Family Group Headquarters, P.O. Box 182, Madison Square Station, New York, New York 10159-0182. There are no dues or membership fees.

Finally, a word of warning is in order. The alcoholic is understandably threatened by anything that undermines his ability to control the people around him and will go to great lengths to prevent his family from attending Al-Anon. He should not be allowed to succeed in these efforts. Family members should attend Al-Anon regardless of the alcoholic's resistance, and they should respond to the alcoholic's increasingly vehement verbal abuse with as much calm and detachment as possible. The alcoholic should be informed that family members are attending Al-Anon to get help for themselves and to learn more about the disease that is making their entire family sick.

STEP 4: Let the Alcoholic Experience the Consequences of His Addiction

Almost every alcoholic suffers from the delusion that he is in control of himself and his drinking. His self-deception is reinforced by family members, friends, and employers or employees who continually shelter him from the consequences of his drunken behavior. This enabling pattern, whether prompted by sympathy, fear, or the need to dominate, is a *natural* and *universal* response to the chaos produced by addiction. Unfortunately, by constantly reducing the crises caused by the alcoholic's drinking, enabling perpetuates the very problem it is meant to solve.

The opportunity to experience the painful results of addictive drinking is a critical step in the alcoholic's recovery process. As long as he can drink *and* lead a reasonably normal life, he will drink. If suddenly he finds himself paying his own fines, cleaning up after himself when he is sick, making his own explanations to his boss, facing bankruptcy, and, if necessary, serving a jail sentence, then he begins to comprehend an important message from reality. His illusion of self-control is shattered, and he learns that he is a desperately sick person whose life is rapidly disintegrating into total chaos. This awareness makes him vulnerable to further efforts to assist him in getting help for his addiction.

For most people, particularly family members, it is not an easy matter to break old patterns of enabling the alcoholic. To stand back and do nothing while the alcoholic suffers genuine pain goes against years of instinctive responses. The practice of "tough love" requires a great deal of prayer, education, and support. And it must be based on the firm understanding that the alcoholic will drink himself to a premature death if he does not get help for his drinking.

Here are several key points to keep in mind when allowing the alcoholic to take responsibility for his own actions.

- *Don't make empty threats.* If you are emotionally unable to carry out a particular non-enabling step, give yourself time to gain courage through prayer and support from Al-Anon friends. The alcoholic has heard empty threats for years, and he is adept at detecting insecurity or equivocation.
- *Don't nag the alcoholic.* Don't allow yourself to be sucked into debates or discussions about his drinking habits. Avoid arguments and fighting. The more quiet strength you demonstrate, the more unsettled the alcoholic will become.
- *Don't hide bottles, pour them out, or measure their contents.* It is impossible to control the alcoholic's drinking by rationing his liquor supply, and attempts

to do so only undermine your efforts to remain emotionally detached.

- *Be honest and open about your actions.* If the alcoholic inquires about the change in your behavior, explain to him that you have learned more about his disease and that you will not be participating in it any longer. Give him literature from Alcoholics Anonymous or Al-Anon, and let him know that help is available if he chooses to seek it. Make sure the alcoholic understands that while you are deeply disturbed by his effort to destroy himself, you have your own life to live and intend to make the most of it.
- *Don't be afraid of losing the alcoholic.* If he threatens to leave, do not try to make him stay. Although he may go away for several days to test your resolve, it is unlikely that he will permanently leave the family he depends on for his basic life needs.
- *Remember that the world is full of enablers.* Don't be surprised if others refuse to join your efforts or if the alcoholic tries to find new enablers among friends, neighbors, or ministers. Some alcoholics must run through a string of enablers before they are finally forced to admit that they are powerless over alcohol.

As family members, close friends, employers, and employees put an end to their enabling actions, the alcoholic will become aware of a new wind blowing in his life. Occasionally, this awareness alone will prompt him to seek help for his drinking. More often, however, a group confrontation or *intervention* is necessary for the alcoholic to take his first step toward recovery.

15

Confrontation

It was late Sunday morning, and Paul Taylor dragged himself out of bed with a groan. He was sick to his stomach, his head hurt, and his hands were shaking. He wished he hadn't had so much to drink the night before, and he was looking forward to a strong cup of coffee.

When Paul came downstairs, he was surprised to find his wife and children sitting in the living room with the family doctor and the vice-president of the insurance company where he was a salesman. The doctor explained to Paul that they wanted to talk with him about his drinking problem, and he asked Paul to take a seat.

It was Paul's wife who spoke first. Her voice was noticeably shaking. "Paul, last Tuesday we went out to dinner for our anniversary and you got drunk," she said. "You poured a bottle of champagne on yourself and made a lewd remark to a woman who passed our table. When the maître d' asked us to leave, you took a swing at him, then passed out on the floor. A busboy helped me put you in the car.

"On our family vacation this summer, you fell asleep while drinking and smoking, and set our cabin on fire. We paid two thousand dollars in damages, and even though we've been going to that camp for fourteen years, the management asked us not to return."

Paul stared at his wife incredulously. He couldn't imagine why she was saying such things in front of his boss and his doctor, but he was too surprised to respond. "Three weeks ago," his wife continued, "you came home drunk in the middle of the night, yelling and swearing. You threw my mother's antique china through the window, and the children and I hid in one of their bedrooms. We were so afraid of what you might do, we locked the door."

Paul glared at his wife and shook his head in amazement. He turned to the vice-president of his company, who was his immediate supervisor, and explained that his wife was a nervous woman who exaggerated problems and frequently became hysterical for no reason. "I may have a little too much to drink now and again," Paul admitted with obvious irritation, "but my wife is really sick. Maybe she needs to see a psychiatrist. You can't imagine the things I've put up with over the years. I should have left a long time ago. Now I'm thinking that I've taken all the abuse I can."

"Dad," Paul's oldest son said hesitantly, "when I was growing up, I was afraid to ride with you in the car. If you had been drinking, you would drive as fast as you could. I thought we were going to be killed. If I asked you to stop, you would laugh at me and tell me to shut up.

"I played football in high school, and I was always afraid of how you would act at my games. One time when you were drinking, you ran out on the field and tried to slug a referee. You yelled obscenities at the teams we played, and I quit during my sophomore year because the other players laughed at you—and at me.

"Last month I brought my fiancée home to meet the family and you were sitting in the rocking chair, drinking. When we were alone you said that you could take her any time you wanted, and that she would like an older man."

Paul was furious. "You're a liar," he shouted at his son. "You've been a troublemaker since the day you were born! If I have a few too many drinks once in a while, it's none of your business. I don't remember inviting you here for a visit. Maybe you should get out before I throw you out!"

Paul jumped up and was heading toward his son when he was intercepted by his boss, who persuaded him to sit down again. Paul made a threatening gesture to his son, but listened to his employer when he spoke. "You're one of our best salesmen," the vice-president said warmly. "And we go back a lot of years. But lately you've cost us three major clients because of your heavy drinking. We want to keep you in the firm, but as long as you are drinking, we can't afford to have you with us."

After the vice-president listed examples of Paul's inappropriate behavior, Paul grew quiet and grim-faced. He slumped down into his chair and listened impassively while his twelve-year-old son explained how worried he was that his father could no longer follow the story line of television shows. "You can't even tell Charlie's Angels apart. You always ask me to explain what's happening, but when I do, you get angry and say I can't talk right. You say I'm stupid."

Paul's seventeen-year-old daughter was the next to speak. She told her father how much she loved him, and how much it hurt that he did not keep his promises. "On my sixteenth birthday, you were going to take me out for dinner, but you came home from work drunk and passed out on the floor. I spend a lot of time at my girlfriend's house, but I never bring her here anymore. I'm afraid she might see you drunk, and I don't know what you will say to her."

The family doctor spoke last. He explained to Paul the physical consequences of his heavy drinking, starting with the damage to his brain and descending to his throat, heart, stomach, and liver. "Your high blood pressure makes you a likely candidate for a stroke," he concluded. "And you are fast becoming permanently impotent because of the shrinking of your testicles. If you continue to drink alcohol, your chances of living another five years are not very good."

When his doctor finished speaking, Paul threw up his hands and looked helplessly at his boss. He admitted that he had been drinking a bit too much and that he was worried about his health. He had been thinking for several months that he should just quit drinking altogether, and now he had made up his mind that's what he would do. "I don't know that you went about it right, saying these things in front of everyone, but at least I get the message. I promise, I've had my last drink, and you won't see me drunk again."

The doctor reminded Paul of all the previous times that he had promised himself to quit drinking, and how difficult it was to stay sober for even a few months at a time. He explained that alcoholism is a disease that does not respond to will power or good intentions. It was highly improbable that Paul would ever stop drinking on his own. But there was a local treatment center which could give him the help he needed. A room was waiting for him, and he could leave in the morning for a thirty-day stay.

Paul admitted that maybe he did need help, but he was offended by the suggestion that he leave immediately. He appealed to his boss to explain that it would take at least a month to find a substitute for his job. The vice-president told Paul that his job was covered, and he was not expected back at work until he completed treatment. This news startled Paul, who protested that he was being railroaded. He wouldn't be pushed around by anyone. He would think it over, and if it seemed like a good idea, he would go when he got ready.

There was an uncomfortable moment of silence, and then Paul's youngest child, a thin, shy five-year-old girl, walked over to her father and put her hand in his. "Daddy," she pleaded, "it's now or never." Paul looked at his daughter and without warning burst into tears. By the next morning he was on his way to a treatment center.

Paul's sudden reversal, as startling as it may seem, was no accident. Rather, it was the expected result of a well-planned and pre-rehearsed confrontation which followed specific rules and guidelines. This guided confrontation, or *intervention,* is a method pioneered by the Johnson Institute in Minnesota, and it has successfully interrupted the downward spiral of addiction for thousands of alcoholics and their families.

The basic structure of an intervention follows a simple pattern. Family members join with other significant people in the alcoholic's life (employers, employees, doctors, ministers, friends) to confront the alcoholic with specific examples of his intoxicated behavior. The atmosphere is loving and nonjudgmental, but firm. As the evidence accumulates, the alcoholic's defense mechanisms give way, and his denial is penetrated. He is forced to admit that he has a serious problem, and for a brief moment, he is open to an offer of outside help.

While the pattern of intervention is simple, carrying out a successful confrontation requires careful planning and professional help. I once attempted a hasty intervention at the request of an impatient family and the result was disastrous. The alcoholic was a close friend of mine, and even before the intervention was underway, he became uncontrollably angry. His threats were so substantial I had to be followed around by the police for several days.

It is family members who suffer the most from a poorly planned intervention. The spiritual battle between light and darkness for an alcoholic can be excruciating, and emotions understandably run high when children are saying things like "Dad, when I brought my fiancée home to meet the family, you told me you could take her any time you wanted." The hostility and anger that spill out of an alcoholic during these times can destroy a family that is not sufficiently prepared.

It takes only one interested person to introduce a family to the intervention method, but before attempting a confrontation, it is important to give careful attention to the following guidelines:

1. *Finding Professional Help.* Every intervention team needs a professional counselor or doctor to supervise its preparation and direct the actual confrontation with the alcoholic. Family members and friends are too emotionally involved with the alcoholic to take the lead themselves; they need a third party who can remain detached even if the situation becomes highly volatile.

To find a qualified counselor who understands the dynamics of both addiction and intervention, concerned persons can call their local drug and alcohol council, or check with Alcoholics Anonymous. In some areas, the medical society can recommend a doctor from the local "Impaired Physicians Committee," a group established to identify and confront doctors who have chemical dependencies. In localities where no trained alcoholism experts are available, information on finding professional help can be obtained from the Johnson Institute, whose address is found in Appendix C at the back of the book.

2. *Choosing the Members of the Intervention Team.* Members of the intervention team are selected on the basis of their close relationships with the alcoholic and their willingness to participate in a confrontation. Not all members of a family will approve of the intervention, but with some education a surprising number will offer to help.

The most strategically important members of the intervention team are the chief enabler (usually a spouse or parent), an employer, and the alcoholic's doctor, if he is knowledgeable about addiction. When available, a recovering alcoholic who is a friend or acquaintance of the alcoholic is also an unusually effective team member. Because the recovering alcoholic has been where the alcoholic now lives, he is able to communicate on a level which is out of reach to non-alcoholics.

Other members of the intervention team can include children, other relatives, close friends, and ministers. There is no age requirement, and small children should not be excluded simply because they are young. Most likely, they are painfully aware of what is happening in their family, and as was the case with Paul Taylor's young daughter, they often make an essential contribution to the intervention.

Individuals who should be *excluded* from the intervention team include: (a) those whose psychological state is too fragile to withstand the emotional impact of confrontation; (b) anyone likely to berate the alcoholic or preach to him in moralistic tones; and (c) family members who

are too full of anger or hate to perceive the alcoholic as a
sick human being in need of help. At the same time, it is
important to remember that there are no perfect members of an intervention team, and seemingly ineffective
people often play important roles. I once selected a
twenty-year-old woman, on the basis of her emotional
maturity and stability, to participate in a confrontation
with her alcoholic mother. During the intervention, the
young woman was so distressed that she cried throughout the entire meeting and was unable to speak a word.
The sight of her capable daughter reacting so emotionally
made such an enormous impression on the alcoholic that
she agreed to enter a treatment program.

In my experience, the optimum number of participants
in an intervention is five or six people, including the professional counselor. It is possible to do an intervention
with as few as two people and, occasionally, with as many
as nine.

3. *Choosing the Data.* In consultation with a professional counselor, each member of the intervention team
selects three or four examples of the alcoholic's inappropriate drunken behavior. These examples need to be as
detailed, current, and colorful as possible, and their focus
should be facts and observations instead of feelings and
judgments. For instance, a statement like "You always
embarrass me in public, and I'm sick and tired of it!" is
better said, "Last month at the Johnsons' party you were
sick all over their new carpet, and here is the cleaning bill
they sent us." Remember that the purpose of this data is
not to humiliate the alcoholic, but to help him see the
true seriousness of his addictive behavior. Angry, hostile
remarks will activate his formidable defense mechanisms,
but evidence given with loving concern enables him to
consider for a moment the truth of the information he
receives.

One member of the intervention team (a doctor if available) needs to inform the alcoholic of the medical consequences of his addiction. My own approach is to start
with the brain and descend down the human body with a

complete list of physical damage. In a one-on-one counseling situation in a doctor's office, the alcoholic normally receives this list as a challenge to prove himself an exception to the rule. In the context of an intervention, he more readily digests the seriousness of his physical decline.

One word of warning: The professional counselor must listen carefully to the history of the alcoholic's behavior as given him by family members. If he detects that there were serious mental problems prior to addiction, it is possible that the alcoholic is using alcohol as medicine for a schizophrenic or other psychotic condition. In such cases, intervention is dangerous and should not be attempted. Instead, if possible, the alcoholic should be directed to a reputable pyschiatrist or mental health institution.

4. *Choosing a Time.* The intervention should be carried out at a time of day when the alcoholic is sober, or as sober as possible. If the intervention team discovers that the alcoholic is drunk at the scheduled hour, the meeting needs to be postponed. In my experience, the Sunday morning after a bad drinking weekend has been an unusually effective time for confrontation. Night meetings, on the other hand, tend to be dangerous and should be avoided if possible.

5. *Holding a Practice Intervention.* Members of the intervention team need to meet at least once, and preferably twice, to rehearse the confrontation. During these meetings the professional counselor plays the role of the alcoholic, and team members practice giving their evidence in a detached, nonjudgmental manner. The "alcoholic" is aggressive and manipulative, and team members are given room for making mistakes and for crying or becoming angry. If the atmosphere of the actual intervention is to be calm and restrained, team members often need this opportunity to ventilate their strong emotions.

Under the counselor's supervision, team members practice responding, or not responding, to the alcoholic's anger and hostility. They prepare for personal attack, rationalizations, the alcoholic's strong sense that he is being

betrayed, and the possibility that he will be falsely compliant ("You're right, I'm an alcoholic. I'm hopeless"; or as
in the case of Paul Taylor, "Maybe I do have a drinking
problem. I'll quit today!"). When team members prepare
in advance for the alcoholic's manipulation and techniques of evasion, it is unlikely that he will catch them off
guard and take control of the intervention.

It is family members who benefit the most from a practice session. They are normally terrified of the coming
confrontation and certain it will fail, but as the rehearsal
progresses they visibly gain confidence and determination. Often it has been years since the family has talked
together honestly, but as each member begins to understand the hurt and bewilderment which other members
have suffered, there is usually a renewal of love and family solidarity. Because of the family's social embarrassment and the alcoholic's ability to "divide and conquer,"
many times family members have not previously shared
with one another specific accounts of the alcoholic's behavior. As they pool their evidence, even the most luke-
warm participants become convinced that the alcoholic is
seriously ill and in need of immediate help.

16

Decision Time

However carefully an intervention team prepares for confrontation with an alcoholic, every intervention is a voyage into the unknown. It is impossible to predict how any individual will respond. Sometimes alcoholics who seem most intractable agree to anything the intervention team recommends, while others who appear highly persuadable offer unexpected resistance. The truth is every alcoholic has his own decision to make, and while the intervention team can learn to control their own behavior, they cannot control the alcoholic.

At the same time, by participating in a confrontation, the intervention team has served notice that there is no going back. They will not continue to support the alcoholic's addiction, and he must choose his next step from a limited number of options. Members of the intervention team need to know in advance what these options are so that they, in turn, can respond appropriately. Accordingly, each team member should ask him or herself the following questions:

QUESTION 1: What if the Alcoholic Agrees to Accept Help?

There is much about a successful intervention which at first glance seems startling and inexplicable. An alcoholic stubbornly committed to drinking, no matter how devastating the consequences, suddenly admits that he has a problem and accepts an offer of help. This reversal is so unexpected that family members frequently have trouble believing the evidence of their own ears.

The key to the alcoholic's sudden change of heart is his own inward torment. While the alcoholic goes to great lengths to appear confident and independent, he is acutely aware of how untenable his position is—he can't live without alcohol, and he can't live with it. He is terrified of his life as an addict, but he is equally terrified at the prospect of losing his supply of alcohol. His growing anxiety is aggravated by his awareness that he cannot take care of himself when he is drinking and by the fear that he will lose the people who support him in his addiction. In order to cope with these escalating tensions, he drinks a chemical which in itself produces the anxiety it is meant to relieve.

When members of the intervention team are able to understand the alcoholic better than he understands himself, they are able to see beyond his hostility and manipulation to the desperation of his heart. Instead of being governed by their own insecurities, they can respond to the alcoholic with loving concern and with an offer for help. This offer frequently appears to be a first glimmer of hope to the despairing alcoholic, and it is likely that he will respond in a positive manner.

There are essentially three options open to the alcoholic who agrees to get help for his addiction, and the intervention team needs to determine in advance which they will suggest for the alcoholic's consideration. These options are:

1. A thirty-day inpatient program at an alcoholism rehabilitation center.
2. An outpatient program at a local alcoholism treatment facility.
3. Attending ninety meetings of Alcoholics Anonymous in ninety days.

Team members should choose a preferred option on the basis of the alcoholic's individual needs, available treatment programs, and financial resources. Alcoholics who have been addicted for years, and whose families are severely damaged by their behavior, do best with options one or two. Alcoholics who have a low level of denial and strong self-motivation may do well with the third option. All three options are discussed more fully in Chapter 18.

If inpatient treatment is recommended, reservations for the alcoholic should be made in advance of the intervention, preferably for the day of, or the day after, the intervention. The less time the alcoholic has to reconsider his decision, the better, and team members should resist his efforts to negotiate a week's or a month's delay. His objections to immediate admission should be anticipated, and arrangements to cover his work responsibilities and other commitments should also be made before the intervention.

QUESTION 2: What if the Alcoholic Refuses Help, but Promises to Quit Drinking on His Own?

Frequently interventions end with the alcoholic refusing to get outside help, but promising that he will quit drinking by his own effort. If, after reasonable efforts to persuade him otherwise, the alcoholic persists in his refusal, the intervention team should take the following steps:

1. *Avoid attacking the alcoholic for his unwillingness to get outside help,* and be thankful for any concession he makes. The level of denial in most alcoholics is so high that under normal circumstances few of them agree to anything, and the public admission of a drinking problem along with a willingness to quit can be a giant first step.

2. *Ask the alcoholic to enter into a verbal or written contract with the intervention team.* In this contract, the team agrees to allow the alcoholic to try to quit on his own, and the alcoholic agrees that if he should drink again, he will get outside help without delay.

Although the alcoholic may sincerely believe that "this time it will be different," it is highly unusual for any addicted drinker to stop drinking on his own. Normally it is only a matter of time before he has a major slip and clearly violates his contract. The non-drinking alcoholic suffers from a torturous condition known as the *dry-drunk syndrome*. His constant physical craving forces him to expend so much energy *not* drinking that he can think of little more than the alcohol he has given up. Because alcohol is still the center of his life, the alcoholic's addictive behavior remains the same, or he becomes even more touchy and irritable than ever. It is impossible for any alcoholic to stay in this state indefinitely. In almost every case, the pressure of his craving will combine with pressures at home and at work to encourage him to try to take just one more drink.

3. Before closing the intervention, *find a way to let the alcoholic know that he is loved,* and that team members sympathize with the struggle his addiction creates. Keep the doors of communication open, and avoid implying that the alcoholic has failed or that he is now rejected by his family or friends.

QUESTION 3: What if the Intervention Fails?

Occasionally an alcoholic storms out of an intervention before it is completed, or refuses to comply in any way with the requests of the intervention team. In such cases, the intervention team should keep in mind the following points:

1. *If possible, try the intervention again.* Occasionally, when a first intervention fails, a second one succeeds.

2. *Don't underestimate the power of time and the alcoholic's own anxiety.* While the alcoholic may appear hardened and unreachable during the intervention, in all likelihood he is hearing and digesting an unsettling amount of information. One of my patients, a young man of eighteen, sat through a New Year's Eve intervention in sullen silence and went out drinking the minute we finished talking. "It was the worst night of my life," he remembers. "For the first time since I became an alcoholic, I knew in my heart what I was doing was wrong. I drank

more than usual, trying to kill the pain I felt, but it wouldn't go away. After two days of drinking, I went into treatment."

3. *Prior to the intervention, think through responses to the alcoholic's potential refusal to get help.* Does the husband or wife plan to stay with the alcoholic? Do the children intend to continue living at home? Does the employer plan to terminate the alcoholic's job? The options available to families are discussed at greater depth in Chapter 22, but it is particularly important for employers to know that they are not doing the alcoholic a favor by keeping him on the job. The mere presence of an employer at an intervention is a powerful incentive for the alcoholic to enter treatment. If the alcoholic grasps the fact that the price of rejecting help is the loss of his job, there is a strong possibility he will rethink his refusal.

4. *Remember that even if the alcoholic never quits drinking, an intervention is almost always a time of healing and reconciliation for family members.* One of the saddest and most difficult confrontations in which I participated was with four teenagers whose parents were co-alcoholics. Their father came close to accepting help for his addiction, but at the last minute was intimidated by threats from his wife. A wealthy uncle who supported the couple participated in the intervention but refused the children's request to stop sending money to their father. The intervention ended when we were thrown out of the house; the children were in tears, and their mother followed us down the road, threatening us all with substantial retaliation. Both parents continued to drink, and within two years, they both died from alcohol-related diseases.

The value of that distressing and seemingly unsuccessful intervention was immeasurable. During the practice session, two of the children discovered that they themselves were addicted—one to cocaine, one to alcohol. Both went into treatment, and today all four children are chemical-free and closely bonded to one another. The children's grandparents, who had been unaware of their tragic home situation, stepped in and provided them with the love and guidance which their parents could not give. And shortly after the intervention, the eldest son came to my office and talked about the mixture of sadness and relief which he felt, now that he had done everything possible for his parents. "I know they probably will never stop drinking," he said. "I'm not happy about the decisions they have made, but I feel like a burden has dropped from my back. My parents' drinking no longer has the power to destroy me. I've done my part, and now I'm free to get on with my own life."

QUESTION 4: What if a Group Intervention Is Not Possible?

Occasionally circumstances arise that make it impossible to carry out a group confrontation. In such situations, it is important to operate with flexibility and creativity. One of my most gratifying interventions involved the simple gesture of giving an alcoholic friend a book about addiction. She read the book, called me for the name of a treatment center, packed her bags, went into a program, and today has been sober for eight years. On another occasion, just prior to a planned intervention, a wife telephoned to say that her husband was threatening me with physical harm if I showed up at their house. The intervention was canceled, but the husband called the following day and angrily demanded to know why his wife was seeing me. I explained that his addiction was a cause for concern, and that there was help available if he was interested. The man agreed to enter a treatment program after Christmas and to my surprise, he kept his promise.

Neither of these examples are given as models to follow, but they illustrate that interventions do not have to be ideal to be successful. Sometimes an unusual moment here or there will break through the alcoholic's denial and bring him or her to the next important step in his recovery process—the willingness to accept outside help.

17

Some Words of Caution

When painful circumstances or an organized intervention compel an alcoholic to seek treatment for his addiction, he and his family members are confronted with important questions: Where does an alcoholic go to learn how to quit drinking? What kind of help does he need?

For many Christians, the answer seems obvious. They are skeptical of efforts to *treat* addiction and convinced that alcoholics find deliverance from alcohol only through repentance and personal conversion. As I travel among church groups, I frequently hear people say, "If only he were right with the Lord; then he wouldn't need alcohol or drugs." The implication is that addiction is strictly a spiritual problem, and that alcoholics and drug addicts who give themselves to God and faithfully attend church services and Bible studies will be cured of their problem.

I identify deeply with this point of view because it was once my own, and I know it often springs from a deep concern and compassion for addicted people. At the same time, I have learned from painful experience that the search for a so-called Christian solution to the problem of addiction usually does more harm than good, and in a sad number of cases, it prevents alcoholics from getting the help they need.

When I first began practicing medicine, I tried to avoid alcoholic patients altogether. Hundreds of unpleasant encounters had taught me that addiction was a hopeless problem, and I preferred not to waste my time with "drunks." Alcoholics I couldn't avoid—those with acute physical symptoms like cirrhosis or bleeding ulcers—I rushed through the standard hospital treatment. They were detoxified with the use of drugs, treated for the most serious of their physical problems, then discharged back into an alcohol-saturated world to await their next physical crisis.

My only success during this period was ridding myself of an alcoholic patient who had aggravated me for years. Henry was an old fraternity friend, and the more he drank, the more he presumed upon our friendship. He constantly pressured me to give him pills for hangovers or admit him to the hospital for imaginary illnesses. His phone calls came at any hour of the day, and he talked continuously of unlucky breaks and lost job opportunities. Finally I had had enough. When Henry called one afternoon, threatening to jump off Nashville's new Memorial Bridge unless I renewed his Valium prescription, I told him to go ahead. He was a pain in the neck, I added, and if he let me know the time of his departure, I would invite our mutual friends. I hung up on Henry without a trace of bad conscience. There were many sick people in the world who *wanted* help; my time was too valuable to waste on patients, or even friends, who were trying to destroy themselves. (Fortunately, Henry did not follow my thoughtless advice and later found help through AA.)

In the early 1970s I went through a revolution in my spiritual life which profoundly affected my attitude toward alcoholics. Like most Southerners from the upper-middle class, I had grown up in an achievement-oriented world of private schools, dance classes, and church services. Except for the months following the death of my father, who was struck by lightning when I was eighteen years old, I maintained a distant, but cordial relationship with God. I called on him when I was in a tight spot and otherwise I relied on my own abilities and professional accomplishments.

Over a period of several years, this optimistic self-reliance began to crumble. My responsibilities as a faculty member of Vanderbilt Medical School were increasing, my private practice was expanding rapidly, and I saw a steady stream of patients whose illnesses did not respond to conventional medicines. These patients, many of whom had consulted numerous specialists, came to the Vanderbilt Medical Center as a last effort to find effective treatment or an accurate diagnosis. Their needs were enormous and far beyond the range of any doctor.

The stark realities of human desperation began to illuminate my own spiritual inadequacy. I needed something to give my patients, but I also needed something for myself. I began to pray for a deeper, more intimate relationship with God, and in time, these prayers were answered. With help from a perceptive patient and a lay renewal ministry within my church, I entered into a new and profoundly personal relationship with God. I surrendered my "M. D.-ity" ego to Jesus and experienced the joy of having his Spirit fill my life.

After this profound conversion experience, I was eager to help my alcoholic patients by leading them into a personal relationship with God. I felt a strong sense of identification with people whose lives were out of control, and I knew that if the Lord could rescue me from the bondage of pride and arrogance, he could rescue alcoholics from the bondage of alcohol. To help my addicted patients surrender their lives to God, I spent a great deal of time sharing my testimony and writing out prescriptions for selected passages from *The Living Bible*. I even handed out copies of the song "He's Got the Whole World in His Hands."

During this time, I saw a string of patients (including three medical doctors) who were bright, gifted, and alcoholic. Despite my good intentions and genuine concern for these patients' spiritual lives, I never cured, or even controlled, a single drinking problem. It was as if my simplistic remedies reduced alcoholism to a spectator's sport. With a diagnosis in one hand and a Bible in the other, I could only stand and watch while my patients exhausted the last energies of their talented lives in pursuit of "just one more drink."

One of these patients was a close friend. Jerry was the toughest, most strong-willed man I had ever met, and our friendship went back many years. I knew that Jerry was a heavy drinker, but by the time his embarrassed family brought him to my office, I had trouble believing the results of my own examination. Jerry's liver was barely functioning, his pancreas was acutely inflamed, and his blood pressure was dangerously high. Jerry spent a week in the detoxification ward, then, in the presence of his wife and children, I warned him that he was going to die in a matter of months if he didn't stop drinking. Jerry was visibly shaken by my diagnosis and vowed never to take another drink. His family promised to do everything in their power to support his decision, and when they left my office I was convinced that Jerry was on the road to a new life.

Jerry's strong will to live, his determination to stop drinking, and the constant love and attention of his family combined to accomplish nothing. And despite my prayers, my *Living Bible* prescriptions, my threats, and my pleadings, Jerry never could stop drinking. For over a year I watched in unbelieving sorrow as this remarkable man involuntarily drank himself to death. It was one of the most anguishing experiences of my medical career. Never again would I dismiss alcoholism as a disease of weak-willed persons.

In the midst of this perplexed helplessness, I attended a week-long workshop at an alcoholism rehabilitation unit in Minnesota. My initial skepticism—What was left to learn that I hadn't already encountered in medical school?—slowly turned to amazement as I watched skilled counselors lead dozens of alcoholics into honest confrontation with their addiction. Many of these counselors were themselves recovering alcoholics who had been sober for ten, twenty, and even thirty years. The key to their sobriety was a twelve-step program which had been in existence since before World War II. Now in every major city and in most small towns there were successful, well-run alcoholic treatment centers or self-help groups whose programs were based on these twelve steps.

It is difficult to communicate the astonishment and regret with which I digested this information. I was a professor of medicine at a major medical university, teaching students the most up-to-date medical science and reluctantly treating numerous alcoholics. All of these patients, as far as I could tell, were drinking themselves to death, and neither I nor my medical colleagues knew of any reliable or medically sound alternative to benign neglect. As a follower of Jesus Christ and a firm believer in the power of the Holy Spirit, I had tried to fill this vacuum by leading my alcoholic patients to conversion, but even the few who recognized their spiritual need were unable to give up drinking.

Now after twenty years of medical practice, I was learning that alcoholism responded to a specific program of treatment, and that over a million men, women, and teenagers all over the world were recovering from addiction. I felt stunned, as if I had spent years unsuccessfully treating diabetic patients with prayer and psychotherapy only to discover that thousands of diabetics were doing quite well by controlling their sugar intake and using insulin. It was a rude awakening.

Today, hundreds of alcoholic patients later, I am more convinced than ever that alcoholism is a treatable disorder. My professional involvement with alcoholics and their families has become one of the most hopeful and inspiring aspects of my medical practice, and while setbacks are unavoidable, the joy of participating in an alcoholic's recovery far outweighs any disappointments I encounter.

Before we examine in detail the treatment options available to alcoholics, there are several important points about the treatment process which need clarification. These include:

1. *No alcoholic should be left alone during the period of physical withdrawal.* Alcohol is a depressant drug and its habitual use results in physical dependence. This dependence is a consequence of the perpetual depression of the central nervous system's normal activity and the adjustments it makes to adapt to the constant presence of alcohol. When alcohol is suddenly withdrawn, the central nervous system rebounds into hyperactivity, and the alcoholic experiences withdrawal symptoms ranging in severity from irritability and nervousness to seizures and delirium tremens (DTs). The most common withdrawal symptom is tremulousness, or "the shakes," which includes an increase in blood pressure, profuse sweating, rapid heartbeat, and sleeplessness. Withdrawal symptoms normally last for two or three days, but they can persist for two to three weeks.

While a few alcoholics have little or no difficulty during withdrawal, the majority of addicted drinkers have physical problems of one kind or another. The severity of their symptoms is usually related to how long and how much the alcoholic has been drinking, but occasionally even short-term drinkers have serious or life-threatening complications. The death rate for unassisted alcohol withdrawal is higher than the rate for heroin withdrawal, and no alcoholic should be alone or without medical supervision during this time. Hospitalization is required for most long-term alcoholics and for any drinker who shows signs of progressing to delirium tremens. The DTs include some of the most acute mental and physical suffering known to man. In this state of withdrawal, the alcoholic's escalating confusion, anxiety, and terrifying hallucinations result in a racing pulse, fever, high blood pressure, uncontrollable shaking, profuse sweating, and a high rate of respiratory and infection problems. Fifteen to 20 percent of alcoholics who suffer from DTs die. There is no reason for withholding medically supervised sedation from any alcoholic who is heading for this potentially fatal state.

Members of Alcoholics Anonymous are often available to sit with an alcoholic during withdrawal, and help can be obtained by calling a local AA chapter. Whether withdrawal takes place in a treatment center, a hospital, or on a rare occasion at home, the alcoholic needs constant reassurance and loving support to help reduce his anxiety and fear. A special effort should be made to explain to him the nature of his symptoms, and the purpose of any necessary medical procedures.

2. *There is no known cure for alcohol addiction.* Alcoholism, like diabetes, is a progressive chronic disorder which can be controlled or arrested, but is seldom cured. While it is thought that a small percentage of alcoholics return to social drinking after developing an addiction, the vast majority of alcoholics, *for the remainder of their lives,* will only control their craving for alcohol by not drinking.

The incurability of alcohol addiction is a stumbling block for some Christians. "I move in full Gospel circles and I believe in healing because I've seen God heal," says an alcoholic friend. "But whenever I tell my friends I'm a recovering alcoholic, they say that's a 'bad confession.' They try to convince me that I'm not *recovering,* I'm *healed.* Sometimes I'm tempted to believe them and have a little glass of wine—after all, other Christians drink socially, why can't I? Then I remember. I *am* an alcoholic. God has healed me from my burning compulsion for alcohol, but all my life I'm going to be just one drink away from a drunk. These friends mean well, but without knowing it, they pose one of the biggest threats to my sobriety."

3. *Instant healings are rare.* There is no question that some people are miraculously and instantly delivered from their physical craving for alcohol. These are the kind of experiences we wish happened frequently, but the truth is that instant healing from addiction is no more common than instant healing from cancer, heart disease, or diabetes. God can heal any of our diseases immediately, but such healings are his business, and as a doctor, I have learned that no one can predict if and when they will occur.

The very real possibility of direct divine intervention does not prevent a doctor from administering God's grace to sick people through medicine and other forms of therapy. *Nor does it excuse the patient from the responsibility of participating in his own health care.* The diabetic waiting for healing is responsible for controlling his diet and, if necessary, for using insulin. The alcoholic, his family members, and his friends have a responsibility to use the tools and principles which are delivering thousands of alcoholics all over the world from the bondage of addiction. To encourage an alcoholic to search for an instant healing while a proven program of recovery is available is a dangerous form of enabling that frequently prevents alcoholics from getting the effective help they need.

In my experience, it is often the case that "instant healings" do well for a couple of weeks or months, and then the wheels start coming off. Even if the recovering alcoholic's physical craving never returns (which is highly unlikely), he is still faced with a host of difficulties. Alcoholism is a wholistic disorder, and both the alcoholic and his family must contend with serious emotional, spiritual, and relational problems connected to addiction. None of these problems will disappear overnight, and we do the alcoholic and his family a grave disservice if we mislead them with a superficial understanding of the Gospel. Without adequate information, they will be unprepared to assess realistically their weaknesses, and they will be caught off guard by persisting problems. At this stage, even alcoholics who have been miraculously delivered from their physical craving often get discouraged and return to a bottle for consolation.

4. *An alcoholic's recovery is usually connected to his ability to perceive his addiction as a disease.* The most common objection to the disease model of addiction is that alcoholics may use it as a means of avoiding responsibility for their drinking. In my experience, this criticism is almost entirely hypothetical; I have never known an alcoholic who rationalized his drinking by blaming it on the *disease* of alcoholism. In fact, the opposite is true. Alcoholics are usually the last people to admit that they have a disease, and it is only when they finally accept this concept that they are able to take constructive steps

toward recovery. "You can't imagine the relief I felt when I learned I had a disease that afflicted millions of people," says one recovering alcoholic. "It was like a burden fell from my back. I wasn't alone anymore. I wasn't paralyzed by guilt, and for the first time in years I thought about the future. I could think through the steps I needed to take to start on the road to recovery." For the majority of alcoholics, the disease model is the means by which they are able to admit to themselves their need for outside help and accept responsibility for the ongoing management of their chronic illness.

18

Paths to Sobriety

The moment of insight which an alcoholic has during an intervention or severe crisis is almost always fleeting. The power of his craving and his well-developed ability for self-deception will propel him back to the bottle if his sense of desperation is not immediately reinforced by a rigorous program of recovery. He has built his life around alcohol; now he must learn to live without it, and his need for reeducation extends to every area of his existence.

Currently there are three well-trodden and successful paths of treatment which help alcoholics find the wholistic healing they need. Some people may be tempted to follow less-tested methods or even paths of their own devising, and perhaps here and there such efforts will be successful. However, recovery statistics side with known treatment programs, and problems as serious as addiction require careful attention to pre-established directions. As one alcoholic said, "If you come to an uncharted minefield and see footprints, you had better follow them—very closely."[1]

OPTION 1: Inpatient Treatment at an Alcohol Rehabilitation Center

Inpatient treatment, which normally lasts a month or more, provides the alcoholic with a structured, simplified environment in which he has few decisions to make and no access to alcohol or drugs. Group meetings, movies, speakers, individual counseling, and spiritual guidance help the alcoholic focus all his energies on a single problem—his addiction. As a combination of loving acceptance and tough confrontation compels the alcoholic toward honest self-assessment, he begins to understand how truly sick he is.

While the alcoholic is coming to terms with his addiction, he is equipped with a variety of tools for learning to resist his craving and live without alcohol. He learns how and when to ask for help. He is taught communication skills, and he begins to recognize in himself and others the difference between manipulation and honest adult communication. He learns how to handle stress, how to talk with his family, how to express his feelings, how to handle disappointment and anxiety without resorting to alcohol, and in general how to practice the whole art of human living which has eluded him since his addiction began. He is helped through the first steps of Alcoholics Anonymous' twelve-step program (see page 140), and he is taught what to expect from his first few difficult months back in society.

The experience of one recovering alcoholic illustrates the momentous choice which faces every alcoholic in treatment. Mary was a devout Christian who became an alcoholic partly in response to a growing strain in her marriage relationship. "During my third week of treatment," Mary remembers, "a counselor asked me in a group meeting what I was going to do if I returned home and found that my problems with my husband were as bad as ever. I said I didn't know. Then she asked me again, and a light went on in my head. I knew what I was going to do. I was going to drink. But as soon as I said this out loud, I realized it didn't have to be that way. I wasn't locked in anymore; I had a choice. Even if my husband never changed, I had tools for sobriety, a support group, and a deepening relationship with God. As it turned out, it was a long time before our home life improved, and I was always grateful for that moment when I learned I was no longer dependent on alcohol."

Today there are hundreds of excellent treatment centers for alcoholics, and a list of accredited programs may be obtained by writing: National Association of Alcoholism Treatment Programs, 2082 Michelson Drive, Suite 200, Irvine, California 92715. It is important to check with local members of Alcoholics Anonymous to receive the inside story on local treatment centers. Any programs under consideration should include a strong family program, prolonged aftercare or follow-up, and a firm commitment to the program of Alcoholics Anonymous.

A twenty-eight day inpatient treatment program usually costs between two and three thousand dollars, but can be as high as thirteen thousand dollars. However, families should not be intimidated or discouraged by this price tag. Most company insurance policies cover alcoholism treatment, and there are many excellent state-run programs whose charges are prorated according to income. Other families may find it worthwhile to borrow money. Treatment for addiction costs less than a good used car, and the potential result is a new life.

OPTION 2: Outpatient Treatment

There are a growing number of outpatient alcoholism treatment centers which provide many of the same programs that are available at inpatient facilities. The guidelines for choosing a reputable institution are the same for both types of treatment centers and, in most cases, costs are comparable.

The advantage of outpatient treatment is that the recovering alcoholic can live at home and does not have to lose time from work. The disadvantage is that there is no controlled environment during the first critical weeks of the alcoholic's recovery. In my opinion, inpatient treatment is preferable except for cases in which the recovering alcoholic's job is threatened by his prolonged absence from work.

For alcoholics who have limited financial resources or who have left their families destitute by years of irresponsible living, there is a third option which provides some of the same resources that are available in a treatment center: attendance at ninety meetings of Alcoholics Anonymous in ninety days.

OPTION 3: Alcoholics Anonymous

In 1935, two hard-drinking alcoholics, whom doctors had long dismissed as hopeless drunks, set out on a bold venture to help each other stop drinking. Four years later, they were surrounded by over a hundred recovering alcoholics, and they could truthfully write about their newly developed program for sobriety:

> Rarely have we seen a person fail who has thoroughly followed our path. Those who do not recover are people who cannot or will not completely give themselves to this simple program, usually men and women who are constitutionally incapable of being honest with themselves. There are such unfortunates. They are not at fault; they seem to have been born that way. They are naturally incapable of grasping and developing a manner of living which demands rigorous honesty. Their chances are less than average. There are those, too, who suffer from grave emotional and mental disorders, but many of them do recover if they have the capacity to be honest.[2]

Today, decades later, Alcoholics Anonymous is a vessel of hope and sobriety for over one million alcoholics in more than eighty countries. An organization which is supported only by voluntary contributions from its members and has no rules, no officers, no "pecking order," no publicity drives, no outside contributions, and no form of promotion save its inherent attraction has become the primary reason why alcoholism today is no longer considered a hopeless condition. Its success is so substantial that every credible addiction treatment center with which I am acquainted owes a large debt to AA and its members.

At the heart of AA's effectiveness is a twelve-step program that gives a systematic account of how the founding members of AA gained their sobriety. These steps are restatements of biblical principles, and while they are simple enough for the foggiest drunk to understand, they are also profound enough that any of us could spend a lifetime trying to practice them without exhausting their spiritual potential. They have been applied effectively to many kinds of seemingly hopeless and compulsive behavior, and they are the reason for the success of Overeaters Anonymous, Gamblers Anonymous, Narcotics Anonymous, Emotions Anonymous, and other such groups.

It is difficult to improve on AA's own introduction to its "Twelve Steps," and much of it is reproduced here. It is my hope that many readers will appreciate the spiritual practicality of these steps and consider their potential healing power not just for alcoholics, but for all of us who struggle to grow in Christian maturity.

> Our stories disclose in a general way what we used to be like, what happened, and what we are like now. If you have decided you want what we have and are willing to go to any length to get it—then you are ready to take certain steps.
>
> At some of these we balked. We thought we could find an easier, softer way. But we could not. With all the earnestness at our command, we beg of you to be fearless and thorough from the very start. Some of us have tried to hold on to our old ideas and the result was nil until we let go absolutely.
>
> Remember that we deal with alcohol—cunning, baffling, powerful! Without help it is too much for us. But there is One who has all power—that One is God. May you find Him now!
>
> Half measures availed us nothing. We stood at the turning point. We asked His protection and care with complete abandon.
>
> Here are the steps we took, which are suggested as a program of recovery:
>
> 1. We admitted we were powerless over alcohol—that our lives had become unmanageable.
> 2. Came to believe that a Power greater than ourselves could restore us to sanity.
> 3. Made a decision to turn our will and our lives over to the care of God *as we understood Him.*
> 4. Made a searching and fearless moral inventory of ourselves.

5. Admitted to God, to ourselves, and to another human being the exact nature of our wrongs.
6. Were entirely ready to have God remove all these defects of character.
7. Humbly asked Him to remove our shortcomings.
8. Made a list of all persons we had harmed, and became willing to make amends to them all.
9. Made direct amends to such people wherever possible, except when to do so would injure them or others.
10. Continued to take personal inventory and when we were wrong promptly admitted it.
11. Sought through prayer and meditation to improve our conscious contact with God *as we understood Him,* praying only for knowledge of His will for us and the power to carry that out.
12. Having had a spiritual awakening as the result of these steps, we tried to carry this message to alcoholics, and to practice these principles in all our affairs.

Many of us exclaimed, "What an order! I can't go through with it!" Do not be discouraged. No one among us has been able to maintain anything like perfect adherence to these principles. We are not saints. The point is, that we are willing to grow along spiritual lines. The principles we have set down are guides to progress. We claim spiritual progress rather than spiritual perfection."*

Members of AA help one another "grow along spiritual lines" through weekly meetings, a one-on-one sponsorship program, and by being available around the clock to answer calls for help from recovering alcoholics who unexpectly find themselves tempted to drink. The atmosphere of an AA meeting is a mixture of loving acceptance, laughter, and the most honest communication I have ever heard. Usually the only masks at AA meetings are worn by visitors or alcoholics who have not yet admitted their addiction. For the rest of the members, the knowledge that they share with one another a dangerous

---

*Portions of Chapter 5 of Alcoholics Anonymous, including "The Twelve Steps," reprinted with permission of Alcoholics Anonymous World Services, Inc.

addiction creates an openness and bond of fellowship that is seldom found in any other area of our society.

The kindness and understanding a visiting alcoholic finds at AA often draws him back to meetings over and over again, even while he continues to mentally disassociate himself from "those crazy drunks." The acceptance he receives from recovering alcoholics revives his dying self-esteem, and over a period of time he finds more and more pieces to the puzzle of his addiction. Veteran members share with him their own struggles with the problems of physical craving, self-deception, paranoia, self-centeredness, and spiritual bankruptcy. When the alcoholic begins to see himself in others, the walls of his denial crumble and he is able to admit that he too is powerless over alcohol.

After an alcoholic admits that his life is unmanageable and turns his life over to God (steps 1, 2, and 3), he begins the hard process of admitting his faults, making restitution to people he has wronged, strengthening his relationship with God, and helping other alcoholics. There are no rules in AA which tell the alcoholic how to carry out these steps, but a large body of collected wisdom and oral history help him make the practical application in his own life. His efforts to help drinking alcoholics continually remind him of the hell from which he has narrowly escaped, and with advice from older members of AA, he learns the art of staying sober "one day at a time."

The great strengths of AA are that it works and it's free. The drawbacks are that AA lacks the multidisciplinary approach of inpatient or outpatient treatment and there is no systematic education about addiction. The information the alcoholic receives depends on the experience of his fellow alcoholics, and while their knowledge is often substantial, in any given AA group there may be blind spots.

Despite these occasional weaknesses, AA is often a reliable alternative to a treatment center, and ongoing participation in its program is an essential part of any alcoholic's recovery. There are AA meetings in all major cities and most small towns, and information on available groups can be obtained by calling local phone listings for

Alcoholics Anonymous or writing to Alcoholics Anonymous World Services, Inc., Box 459, Grand Central Station, New York, New York 10163.

The success of AA is based on principles, not personalities. If an alcoholic is bothered by certain individuals in his group, he can change groups or learn to put up with people he doesn't like for the sake of his sobriety. Every alcoholic should be encouraged to attend at least six meetings of AA before deciding on its usefulness, and he should be reminded that it isn't necessary for him to like the meetings. There are many areas of life in which we must carry out responsibilities whether we like them or not, and for the alcoholic, attending meetings of AA is one of these areas. In most cases, an alcoholic's refusal to attend AA is rooted in his pride and embarrassment. After sticking with it for a few months, however, he is likely to find that AA has become the highlight of his week.

Alcoholics Anonymous and the Christian Believer

Despite AA's unparalleled success with alcoholics, some Christians avoid participating in its program because of its seemingly vague spirituality and the use of phrases such as "Higher Power" and "God as you know Him." These people are convinced that the only bona fide recovery programs are those that name the name of Jesus, and when Jesus doesn't specifically get credit for the alcoholic's sobriety, they have trouble believing that the recovery is legitimate.

From my perspective as a physician, this view is shortsighted and prevents many people from getting the assistance they need. Alcoholics Anonymous has helped thousands of alcoholics from all religious persuasions, and Christian alcoholics have no trouble understanding the "Higher Power" as the Lord Jesus. I have never known any alcoholic whose faith was damaged by the spiritual program of AA, but I know dozens of Christians who first committed themselves to Jesus Christ because of their contact with Christian AA members and because of the spiritual progress they made by following "The Twelve

Steps." As one recovering alcoholic told me, "Alcoholics Anonymous won't get you to heaven, and it can't keep you out of hell, but it can keep you sober long enough to make up your own mind."

Historically speaking, alcoholics repeatedly turned for help to the helping professions, to doctors and ministers, and received no help at all. So, out of desperation, they turned to one another, and from their fellowship and mutual support came Alcoholics Anonymous. Out of this group of people whom everyone else dismissed as completely hopeless, AA has produced hundreds of thousands of recovering alcoholics, and the testimony of these transformed lives cannot be rejected out of hand.

In my own experience, with few exceptions, a person first must be sober before he can hear or practice the Gospel. I have a friend, a born-again surgeon and an alcoholic, who refused to go to Alcoholics Anonymous and tried to get sober by going to Bible studies and prayer meetings. Although he explained his decision in spiritual terms, his primary motivation was that he didn't want to admit that he was just like all those other "drunks." He never could stop drinking. Finally he humbled himself, admitted that he was powerless over his addiction, and worked "The Twelve Steps" of AA. Today he is back at Bible studies and prayer meetings, and he is a faithful if somewhat humbler servant of God.

Having said all this, a word of warning is in order. Occasionally some members of Alcoholics Anonymous develop the "AA is all there is" syndrome. Although at certain stages of recovery, it is natural for alcoholics to make AA the center of their lives, as time goes on it is important that this program be put in its proper perspective. The founders of Alcoholics Anonymous were careful to emphasize that they were operating only a "spiritual kindergarten," and Christian recovering alcoholics need to make sure they do not mistake the rescue boat for dry land. For the Christian, Alcoholics Anonymous is an effective means to an end, and that end is not a program of recovery or fellowship with other alcoholics, but a sober life lived to the glory of God.

19

When the Honeymoon Ends

Philip Adams began drinking alcoholically at the age of sixteen. For the next twenty-two years, alcohol was the center of his life. He drifted in and out of marriage, through mental hospitals and treatment centers, and occasionally attended meetings of Alcoholics Anonymous. One year he had a conversion experience at a small community church, but before long he was drinking more heavily than ever. Disowned by his family and convinced that God had permanently rejected him, Philip slid ever more deeply into despair. He began living on the streets, panhandling for drinking money, sleeping in alleys, and eating whatever food he could find. For seven years, his only address was skid row; his only friends were street drinkers.

In 1972, an extraordinary chain of events radically altered Philip's life. While trying to con his way into a job for which he had no qualifications, he met and fell in love with a devout Christian woman. He began attending church, and one Sunday during a communion service, he experienced the transforming power of Jesus Christ. Within six months, Philip was married, he had a home and car, and he was doing exceptionally well in a prestigious law school. His years on skid row quickly became a distant memory, and his future seemed endlessly bright.

Philip's astonishing transformation made him an instant hero in his church and within a short time he was

elected to the office of deacon. This was just the beginning in a whole series of new responsibilities which he
accepted as a husband, a father, and a lawyer. He put two
children from a previous marriage through college and
assumed care of a teenage daughter. Within a few years
after graduating from law school, he had his own law firm
and a rapidly expanding practice. He felt deeply his responsibility for his clients' lives and property problems.
His phone rang at all hours of the night, and he was always willing to lend a listening ear to anyone in trouble.
Because he had been on the bottom himself, he was eager
to share with others the secret of his new life.

Philip's gift for counseling, his extraordinary professional accomplishments, and his rapid rise to prosperity
and influence concealed serious gaps in his emotional development. "I was healed and could do no wrong," remembers Philip. "I looked good and sounded good, and
everyone assumed I knew what I was doing. In fact, after
twenty-two years of addiction, I had no idea how adults
handled responsibility, and I had the emotional maturity
of a teenager. I was absorbed in myself. I had to have
everything I wanted right away, and I seldom thought
about the future consequences of my actions. I wasn't
drinking anymore and I didn't live on skid row, but in
almost every way I still thought and acted like an alcoholic."

Philip felt increasingly trapped by his enormous, always
expanding responsibilities, and he slowly slid into self-pity
and depression. He began to resent his wife for her role in
his business success, and he looked to the future with
dread and insecurity. He felt as controlled by outside circumstances as he did when he was living on the street,
but now there was no alcohol to relieve his fears or bol-
ster his flagging self-esteem. Why had God given him a
job and family he couldn't handle? Why had he allowed
someone with his shameful past and inabilities to advance
so rapidly? Philip began to fantasize that he was back on
skid row where his only worry had been where to find his
next drink. If only he could solve his problems as easily as

he had in the past. One bottle and he could forget everything!

Five years after his last drink, feeling desperate and
helpless, Philip visited his doctor to complain of insomnia
and job-related tensions. The physician recommended a
vacation and wrote out a prescription for a month's supply of Valium. The pills were immediately effective, and
Philip was astonished at how quickly his anxieties disappeared. He was no longer intimidated by his own accomplishments; he couldn't remember why his responsibilities
were so upsetting; and his conflicts with his wife seemed
unimportant. For the first time in years, he felt confident
and relaxed, ready to face whatever the future might
bring.

Within six months, Philip had a new problem—he was
addicted to Valium. He visited a different doctor every
week to get a month's supply of pills, and the awareness
of his new addiction filled him with self-hatred and despair. When he imagined himself back on skid row, it was
no longer a pleasant fantasy but a frightening possibility.
Week by week he was becoming less and less able to
practice law, and his home life was deteriorating rapidly.
At times he was certain he had been cast out forever from
God's family; at other times, he questioned God's existence and wondered if all the miracles of his life had been
products of wishful thinking and group enthusiasm. He
desperately wanted help, but his position in his church
and his community prevented him from sharing his need
with others.

For a second time, Philip's wife intervened and set in
motion the chain of events which freed her husband from
addiction. She contacted a Christian counselor who assured Philip of the continued love of Christ and directed
him to a psychiatrist who understood the dynamics of
alcoholism and other drug addictions. Through intense
prayer, education, family counseling, and three hospital-
izations, Philip was finally delivered from his physical and
psychological dependence on Valium.

Today, Philip knows that his second addiction devel-

oped as a logical conclusion to ways of thinking and acting that grew out of his twenty-two years of compulsive
drinking. "I had never grown up," says Philip. "I responded to everything on the basis of my feelings, and it
never occurred to me that I could have strong emotions
and not act on them. At the age of forty-six I had to learn
the patience that most people learn as young adults. It
took me a long time to accept the fact that there are
roadblocks and difficulties that may last as long as life
itself and that as human beings we will always be subject
to feelings of pain and discouragement. Now I know that
the challenge of life is not to escape difficulty, but to see
God's grace at work even if old feelings return and circumstances refuse to change. Then, as our experience accumulates, we come to know that whatever happens to
us, we grow in grace and see more and more of God's
glory."

As Philip came to grips with his own insecurities and
immaturity, he grew more tolerant of the weaknesses of
others and less inclined to pass judgment on those who
failed. He also hired an answering service to take night
calls and began to refer clients with serious spiritual and
psychological difficulties to pastors and professional
counselors. "There was a lot of pride mixed up in my desire to help my clients straighten out every area of their
lives," recalls Philip. "Today, I still care for people deeply,
but I take a more professional attitude and am more
aware of my own limitations. I can handle legal problems,
but there are other people who do a better job at counseling and pastoral ministry."

At the heart of Philip's changing relationship with his
clients was his deepening relationship with God and a
growing understanding of what it means to be a follower
of Jesus Christ. "After I sobered up, I paid lip service to
the concept of grace, but unconsciously I was convinced
that everything depended on me. It was an incredible relief to realize that it was not me, but *Christ in me* who
accomplished the work of God's kingdom. I could do all
things *through Christ,* and I could be prompted to action
by the Holy Spirit instead of by my fear of failure. It was

only when I understood these spiritual truths that I was able to accept my legitimate responsibility for my family and my clients."

The story of Philip Adams, while unusual in the extremity of its peaks and valleys, follows a pattern which is found again and again in the lives of recovering alcoholics. In almost every case, the first weeks or months of sobriety are a period of rapid change and exhilarating progress. The newly sober alcoholic wakes up in the morning without a headache, his hands are steady, and he can eat without vomiting. His mind works more quickly than it has in years, and he no longer has to worry about blackouts or lost weekends. Although in the back of his mind there is a nagging fear that this period of sobriety will end like all the others—with a drink—his confidence and self-esteem are reinforced with each sober day. The joy he feels bears a distinct resemblance to the euphoria he experienced during his early drinking days. He is "high" on being sober, and he thinks and acts with the reckless abandon of a new convert.

Sooner or later, for every recovering alcoholic, the honeymoon comes to an end. For some it dies abrupty when, from out of nowhere, their physical craving for alcohol returns with a staggering intensity. For others, like Philip Adams, there is a gradual but often shattering confrontation with old problems and new responsibilities. The recovering alcoholic is handicapped by past resentments and rationalizations, by echoes of self-pity, and by a physical fatigue and lethargy that may last for a year or more after withdrawal. Family relationships are often rocky, wives or husbands who have held up admirably during the alcoholic's drinking days may suddenly collapse emotionally, and angry children may take revenge for the years they have suffered with an unfeeling, unrepentant alcoholic parent. Everywhere the recovering alcoholic looks, there are fences to mend and bridges to build, and often he cannot remember exactly how or why his relationships have been broken.

While the newly recovering alcoholic tries to solve the problems his addiction has created, he must also relearn the art of everyday living. As a drinker, he surrendered many if not most of his adult responsibilities. Now, he must learn again to pay bills, to share household tasks, to care for children, to organize his time. Recovering alcoholics frequently have no idea how long it takes sober people to accomplish a given job; they may set aside two hours to paint an entire house, or a whole day to run a half-hour errand.

In many ways the recovering alcoholic is like an amnesia victim, a chemically created Rip Van Winkle who returns to life five, ten, or even forty years later to discover that a large segment of his adult life has disappeared. There are deaths he never mourned, celebrations and weddings in which he never participated, perhaps even criminal behavior about which he never worried. He may be overwhelmed with grief when he realizes how much of his life has been drowned in alcohol—the energy of his young adulthood will not return and there are lost years with family members, particularly children, which can never be recovered.

The newly sober alcoholic who faces the multiple burdens of private grief, family problems, and adult responsibilities is almost always handicapped by immaturity and inadequate emotional development. Maturation ends when addiction begins, and the child, teenager, or adult who learns to solve his problems by swallowing a chemical falls far behind his peers in wisdom and the ability to handle difficulties. Philip Adams became an alcoholic at the age of sixteen. Twenty-two years later, when he finally sobered up, he had missed critical stages of human development. He still thought and acted like a teenager. Unlike alcoholics who become addicted later in life, he had few learned adult behaviors to which he could return, and he had little experience in handling anxiety and pressure without drinking. He was used to quick answers and shortcuts, and he had yet to test his abilities and his perceptions of himself against the realities of life.

At the same time, the problems Philip had created for

himself were complex and troubling enough to push even the most resourceful adults to their spiritual and psychological limits. It was no accident that, like many other recovering alcoholics, Philip began to romanticize his drinking days and recall with regret the pleasures of intoxication. He was still secretly convinced that it was only alcohol which made life worth living. As he reflected on the long dry years ahead, it no doubt seemed as if by giving up alcohol he was burying one of his dearest and most dependable friends.

It should be obvious by now that simply *not drinking* is not enough to keep a recovering alcoholic sober. If he does not learn to handle difficulties, and if he continues to look for a quick fix to all of life's problems, he will almost inevitably return to his dependence upon alcohol or develop a new addiction to another drug. If the recovering alcoholic is to remain sober, he must learn that it is unrealistic and dangerous to seek to live each day in a cloud of euphoria, and he must pay careful attention to the guidelines for recovery which have enabled other alcoholics to survive the pitfalls of sobriety.

20

Guidelines for Recovering Alcoholics

It is said that the navy's book of safety regulations for the high seas was written item by item as a result of the deaths of sailors—when lives were lost, a rule was born. The guidelines governing the behavior of recovering alcoholics have much the same history. They are a result of years of experience, and they serve as signal lights to direct the recovering alcoholic to safe waters, while helping him avoid the dangerous shoals where many other men and women have met disaster.

Most newly sober alcoholics are strongly tempted to think of themselves as exceptions to the rule, and family members and other concerned persons should take care not to encourage this illusion. Most "exceptions" end up drinking again, and their failure to remain sober is usually directly related to their unwillingness to follow the example of other recovering alcoholics.

The guidelines which follow do not exhaust the wealth of information available to a recovering alcoholic through treatment centers and Alcoholics Anonymous, but they serve to highlight some of the potential dangers which face the newly sober alcoholic.

1. *Avoid old drinking friends.* It is all too easy for a recovering alcoholic to walk out of a treatment center and into the arms of his former drinking buddies. The seductive nature of these relationships cannot be overem-

phasized. While teenagers are particularly susceptible to peer pressure, even grown adults may find themselves longing for the camaraderie and false sense of fellowship generated by shared intoxication.

Jeff was a friendly, outgoing thirty-three-year-old when I first met him in the intensive care unit of our hospital. He had been admitted while in an alcoholic coma and was bleeding so severely from his esophagus, that I didn't expect him to live. But he genuinely wanted help, and when his condition unexpectedly improved, he agreed to enter a treatment center. His family gave him a one-way ticket to an excellent rehabilitation unit, but two weeks later he was back in Nashville, hanging out at his favorite bar. His drinking buddies had taken up a collection and sent him a bus ticket home. Frightened by the responsibilities of sobriety and tempted by the thought of old familiar friends, Jeff accepted their offer and was soon drinking more heavily than ever. The next time we met, he was again in the critical care unit, paralyzed from the waist down as a result of a drunk-driving accident.

A number of alcoholics are also involved in destructive relationships with husbands, wives, parents, or friends who, whether consciously or unconsciously, try to control the alcoholic by keeping him drunk. A husband who is threatened by a newly sober wife may attempt to persuade her that she is more attractive when she drinks; a friend of a recovering alcoholic may insist again and again that "one drink never hurt anyone." The recovering alcoholic must distance himself from these unhealthy relationships as far as circumstances allow. Maintaining sobriety is his number one priority, and not even the deepest of friendships or family ties should be permitted to stand in his way.

2. *Maintain AA Attendance.* In the excitement and euphoria which surround the early days of recovery, it is easy for newly sober alcoholics to convince themselves that, while others need AA, they will do perfectly fine without it. "I came out of a great treatment program on a real high," remembers one young Christian student. "I

felt closer to the Lord than ever before, and I became
deeply involved with a campus fellowship group. I knew I
didn't need AA and all that 'Higher Power' stuff; with God
on my side, what could I learn from a bunch of old
drunks? Before I knew what hit me, I was drunk again. I
finally figured out that there is more to recovery than
saying 'let God handle it,' and I started going to AA. Now,
little by little, I'm getting to where I want to be."

While it is true that some alcoholics stay sober without
attending AA, thousands of men and women have died
trying to prove that they should be included in this number. To ignore the program of Alcoholics Anonymous or
to abandon it early in the recovery process is to throw
away the most successful support system available for
recovering alcoholics. "Trying to stay sober over the
years without AA is like trying to get to heaven without
identifying with a church," says one veteran alcoholism
counselor. "That's the hard way."[1]

3. *Easy does it.* Through years of compulsive drinking,
the recovering alcoholic has accustomed himself to the
instant gratification of needs and desires. When he sobers
up, he often attempts to make up for the time he has lost
to drinking by trying to solve all his problems at once. He
is easily distracted by irrelevant issues, has an instant answer for every question, and is deeply discouraged when
confronted with obstacles. James, a recovering alcoholic,
says, "It's the alcoholics who try to set the world on fire
who drink again. If you don't learn patience, you're as
good as gone. When I was drinking, I had to have everything yesterday. Now, I know how to wait, and if I have
to wait all my life for what I want, I will."

Family members, friends, and ministers should likewise
exercise caution in their expectations for the recovering
alcoholic. Philip Adams was appointed a deacon in his
church shortly after his first year of sobriety, and the
trauma of this responsibility played a significant factor in
his second addiction. "If I had been more mature, I never
would have accepted the position," he says today. "But
the expectations of the people in the church were very

high. They believed I could do it, and their confidence fed my pride and my alcoholic need for instant gratification."

Whenever possible, recovering alcoholics should keep life simple and avoid making dramatic changes in their employment, marital status, or geographical location for at least a year after they become sober. They and their families should also keep in mind that, during the recovery process, other compulsive behavior cannot be eliminated overnight. For example, alcoholics who smoke should usually wait six months to a year before trying to give up cigarettes. Although smoking cigarettes is as damaging to physical health as addictive drinking, there are very few people who can cope successfully with the strain of battling two addictions at once.

4. *Avoid mood-altering drugs.* Every year thousands of alcoholics like Philip Adams inadvertently trigger the return of their craving for alcohol by ingesting mood-altering drugs. Some fall victim to uninformed doctors who too freely write prescriptions for tranquilizers or pain pills. Others use weight control pills, swallow cough syrup, or take seemingly harmless decongestants. Because mood-altering drugs easily substitute for one another, and because many leading over-the-counter drugs contain alcohol, recovering alcoholics must be extraordinarily cautious in their use of medicine. On the following page, there is a partial list of those drugs which should be avoided, but before taking any medicine, recovering alcoholics should make a safety check with an informed alcoholism counselor. Most recovering alcoholics have a low threshold of pain. They are accustomed to medicating themselves for every physical and mental discomfort, and now they must retrain themselves to let colds, headaches, and other minor illnesses run their course.

For their part, doctors who prescribe mood-altering drugs must do so with care, only after taking a thorough patient history. Several years ago I had a patient who came to me complaining of "nerves" and insomnia. His nine-year-old son had been killed several years earlier by a drunk driver. The father himself had picked pieces of

Drugs and the Alcoholic

The following is a partial list of drugs which experience has shown to be hazardous to alcoholics and other chemically dependent people:

- All sedatives, including barbiturates and synthetic drugs. Barbiturates such as Nembutal, Seconal, Tuinal, etc., and synthetic sedatives such as Doriden, Quaalude, Dalmane, Placidyl, etc.
- All narcotics, including opium derivatives such as codeine, morphine, heroin; and synthetic narcotics, such as Demeral, etc.
- All tranquilizers, including the newest ones. Of special danger are Valium and Librium due to their wide usage and addiction capabilities.
- Most pain-relieving medications such as Darvon, Talwin, etc. Darvon seems to act as a tranquilizer, and Talwin has characteristics of a narcotic. Both these drugs are capable of producing severe addictions.
- All antihistamines.
- The drugstore medications containing antihistamines, or scopolamine, such as Nytol, Sominex, Contac, Dristan, NyQuil, and even Miles Nervine.
- Antidepressants and stimulants such as Elavil, Ritalin, and amphetamine compounds, etc.
- Cough medicines and other medications containing narcotics, alcohol, or antihistamines. This means almost *all* cough syrups and *many* liquid vitamin preparations.
- Weight-control tablets.
- Reserpine compounds, which are basically tranquilizers. Preparations containing reserpine prescribed for hypertension should be used with caution and only when absolutely necessary.

the broken steering wheel out of the boy's body. The man had never recovered from his grief, and now he needed help sleeping. I gave him a month's supply of sleeping pills, but four days later his wife called back for a refill. "My husband is acting just like he did when he was addicted to alcohol," she said with alarm. I immediately canceled the man's prescription and fortunately no harm was done, but my oversight could easily have led to disaster.

A further word of caution is in order. The majority of alcoholics today are cross-addicted to one or more drugs—cocaine, marijuana, tranquilizers, hallucinogens, amphetamines—and it is important that all recovering alcoholics understand that they cannot stay sober and continue to use other addictive substances. Many young alcoholics in particular try to convince themselves that they can abstain from alcohol and still use cocaine or marijuana occasionally. In fact, these drugs are interchangeable with alcohol and, in almost every case, they will lead the recovering alcoholic back to drinking within a few days or weeks.

5. *Learn to cope with painful emotions.* A drinking alcoholic is cut off from his own internal pain by the depressing qualities of alcohol and by his own skillful use of rationalization, projection, and denial. After years of living with numbed and suppressed emotions, he has little memory of the strength of unmedicated human pain. When he suddenly stops drinking, he is often caught off guard by the force of his negative feelings—anger, sadness, embarrassment, anxiety, and resentment. Of these, it is resentment which is the most dangerous. "This business of resentment is infinitely grave," writes the founder of Alcoholics Anonymous. "We found that it is fatal. For when harboring such feelings we shut ourselves off from the sunlight of the Spirit. The insanity of alcohol returns and we drink again. And with us, to drink is to die."[2]

It is essential that the recovering alcoholic learn to accept a certain amount of emotional pain as a natural part of life and to separate his negative feelings from a desire to drink. In the past he had translated emotional reactions such as, "I'm angry at my wife," into "I need a drink." Now, the alcoholic must learn healthy, adult ways of identifying his feelings and coping with them. His education begins at treatment and continues with the twelve-step program of AA.* Many recovering alcoholics also find it helpful to have one-on-one counseling with a professional who can help them identify their emotions and learn to communicate with others in an adult manner.

6. *If the craving returns* . . . Six months, five years, or three decades after his last drink, it is possible for the recovering alcoholic to experience a sudden and unexpected return of his physical craving for alcohol. It is important that the recovering alcoholic be aware of this possibility and that he not equate the return of his craving with failure. He is no longer a helpless victim, and he can resist temptation by responding to it properly. Important steps to take during this period include:

- Step up participation in Alcoholics Anonymous.
- Talk over the experience with other recovering alcoholics. Don't pretend the craving isn't there, and don't underestimate its power.
- Take seriously the Bible's command to "flee from sin." Under normal circumstances recovering alcoholics can attend restaurants and parties where alco-

---

*I know of no better way for handling resentment than the method found in the "Blue Book" of Alcoholics Anonymous. It is suggested that the recovering alcoholic make a list of the people he resents, specify their hurtful action, and identify why he felt threatened by them. He then makes a list of his own faults and fears, and honestly admits his wrongs to other people. After he has done this, it is easier for him to see that the people who have offended him are no different than himself; they are people who need tolerance, patience, and pity. The recovering alcoholic asks God to give him this tolerance and kindness, and to show him a way that he can be helpful to the person who has wronged him.[3]

hol is served, but during this vulnerable time it is best to avoid situations where drinks are readily available.

- Consider taking Antabuse only under the direction of a physician. Antabuse is a drug which interacts with alcohol to make a drinker violently ill. It is not a cure for addiction, but alcoholics find it effective in conjunction with treatment. Some take a half pill daily for their entire life as an extra safeguard against an impulsive drink. Antabuse is effective for up to four or five days after ingestion and allows the alcoholic time to get a hold on his craving. Persons taking Antabuse must be careful to avoid all medications containing alcohol; the risks of mixing alcohol and Antabuse include serious convulsions and death.

For recovering alcoholics who take proper precautions, maintain their humility, attend AA, and practice the twelve-step program, there is the joyous prospect of living alcohol-free for the rest of their lives. If their family members and close friends are to join in this celebration of sobriety, it is essential that they too recognize their need for help and commit themselves to a recovery program.

21

Family Recovery

When Jack arrived at the local Presbyterian church, asking for help, he was bankrupt, homeless, and unemployed. A former millionaire, he had lost everything he owned during a fifteen-year drinking spree. Now, he was in the early stages of recovery from alcoholism, and as a husband and father of five children, he was requesting temporary financial help from the church.

The pastor and other church members responded to Jack's need immediately and provided him with a home, a job, and a car. Jack was deeply moved by the love he received and with encouragement from new Christian friends, he renewed his commitment to Jesus Christ. He became an active church member, and he and his entire family attended services three times a week. Within a few years, Jack was elected to the board of deacons.

While Jack continued to make remarkable progress in all areas of his life, his wife, Beth, became increasingly quiet and withdrawn. One day she visited the pastor, complaining of depression and loneliness. "No one knows what it's like for me," she said bitterly. "My husband ruined my life and the lives of my children by drinking away our money, and now I'm left to pick up the pieces. Everyone thinks he's so terrific because he's a recovering alcoholic, but they don't have to live with his mistakes. Maybe if I were an alcoholic, someone would think about me for a change."

The pastor was surprised at the depth of anger which Beth expressed. Assuring her that she too was loved and admired, he urged her to forgive her husband and to guard against self-pity. Beth seemed untouched by this appeal, and two months later she returned to the pastor's office to say that she herself was now drinking alcoholically. The pastor, dismissing her claim as a bid for attention, tried to help her address her own anger and resentments.

Several weeks later, the pastor discovered that Beth had told him only half the truth. Not only was she drinking alcoholically, she was also having an affair with another alcoholic. "After a bad weekend binge, Beth agreed to enter a treatment center," remembers the pastor, who is now my own minister. "But she had far more difficulty giving up alcohol than her husband. She suffered from repeated relapses, and finally she and Jack were divorced. When I last heard from them, Jack was sober, but Beth was still drinking.

"My mistake was that I failed to recognize that alcoholism is a family affair. As a church, we heaped attention on Jack, with good results, but we failed to give his wife the same support and encouragement. She had lived through hell with her husband, but we never noticed her deep pain until it took an outward form that was too obvious to be ignored. Unfortunately, by that time, it was too late."

One of the most damaging myths that surrounds addiction is the belief that if the alcoholic stops drinking, his family's problems will disappear. The popularity of this misperception is one of the main reasons that the divorce rate among alcoholic families is higher *after* the alcoholic is recovering than when he is drinking. The truth is that patterns of relationships and behavior which have been going on in a family for years do not disappear overnight. Unresolved problems threaten not only marital relationships and the stability of individual family members, but in many cases, they contribute to the recovering alcoholic's decision to return to drinking.

The problems which face the family of a recovering alcoholic can be overwhelming. Although family members are normally happy that the alcoholic is sober, they live in fear that his drinking will begin again at any moment. If he comes home late, they smell his breath. If he's depressed, they worry that they have done something which will make him drink. There are often legal and financial battles to fight, and past resentments and hurts make it hard to forgive and forget. Old patterns of communication remain, and family members may be unable to talk with one another without resorting to familiar modes of nagging, criticism, or manipulation. Furthermore, the recovering alcoholic is likely to be preoccupied with himself and his recovery. He often becomes too involved with meetings and new friends to give proper attention to his family. He may speak in a jargon that others find incomprehensible, and his growing sense of self-worth may aggravate his marriage partner's already substantial insecurities.

If family members are to overcome these difficulties, it is essential that they make use of family counseling resources and that they follow their own program of recovery. They must also keep in mind two important points:

1. The family can get well whether or not the alcoholic stops drinking.
2. While ideally the family which gets sick together, gets well together, in reality, individual family members move at their own pace and they must give each other time to deal in their own ways with the difficulties they face.

The following steps are among the most important that family members can take toward their own recovery.

STEP 1: Identify the Problems

Most family members of alcoholics have spent years ignoring their emotions and the reality of their own inter-

nal tensions. As a result, they have grown increasingly
out of touch with themselves and each other. Often they
have progressed to a stage in which they are no longer
able to assess the severity of their psychological and spiritual problems. They need outside observers, whom they
can trust, to help them identify their difficulties and learn
to cope with problems in ways which lead to healthy personality development. This help is available from Al-
Anon, Alateen, and special community groups for adult
children of alcoholics, as well as from professional counselors trained in the dynamics of both addiction and family relationships. Family members should commit themselves to working "The Twelve Steps" of Al-Anon, and
whenever finances allow, they should seek help *as a unit*
from a family counselor. The problems of family members
are interconnected and feed on one another, and it is extremely helpful when they are able to sit down with an
objective third party and face their difficulties together.

As we have seen, children and adult children of alcoholics have special problems to overcome. They must learn
to cope with the damage that was inflicted during their
critical years of development, and many of their wounds
have become essential ingredients of their character. Self-
reliance has been one of their most effective tools for survival, and it is extremely difficult for them to ask for, or
accept, outside help. Their friends and family members
will need patience and persistence to encourage these exceptionally hurt individuals to seek the help they need.

STEP 2: Avoid Unrealistic Expectations of the Recovering Alcoholic

False expectations and disappointments are among the
most dangerous traps which face the family of a recovering alcoholic. In the early months of recovery, family
members often swing back and forth between extreme
pessimism and extreme optimism as they adjust their
hopes and fears to the realities of living with their particular alcoholic. While the alcoholic was drinking, many

family members lived in a fantasy world where all their problems were solved by his recovery, and it is often shattering to discover that he is still a difficult person to live with even when he is sober. In fact, the recovering alcoholic may be more touchy and irritable than ever. It is often months before he is capable of consistent and mature adult behavior.

For the sake of emotional survival, the joy which accompanies the alcoholic's sobriety must be tempered with the realization that frustrations and setbacks are a natural part of the recovery process, and that the alcoholic and his family need to make recovery the focus of their efforts for two or more years. Like the recovering alcoholic, family members must learn to take one day at a time, to set realistic goals, and to avoid sudden changes. They must learn to expect difficulty as a given of life, and they must avoid thinking of Al-Anon or professional counselors as people who can offer a cure-all for family problems. In reality, such therapy is designed to give family members tools with which they can work out their own recovery. It is the family members themselves who must face the challenging task of applying these tools to their own lives and circumstances. No outsider can make a family well, and concerned friends and church leaders must be careful not to encourage misplaced responsibility or unhealthy dependency.

STEP 3: Surrender the Past

Kate was eleven years old when her alcoholic father died from cirrhosis of the liver. Her mother, whose emotional stability had been undermined by years of living with a happy but irresponsible drunk, plunged into a deep depression and tormented her daughter with erratic and inexplicable behavior. There were unexpected slaps, screaming fits, endless accusations, and days of morbid silence. Because of her mother's increasing helplessness, Kate assumed responsibility for the family finances and household chores. When her mother became jealous of the time she spent studying and began tearing up homework assignments, Kate learned to study outdoors on the street. Despite her mother's interference, Kate was an outstanding student, but her dream of a college education died when her mother became a bedridden invalid. In order to pay household bills, Kate went to work in a bank.

In her early thirties, after marriage and four children, Kate became a Christian through a neighborhood Bible study group. A responsible, disciplined person who never lost self-control, she quickly established herself as an excellent leader and organizer. She grew rapidly in her knowledge of Scripture, and she had a deep sense of spiritual responsibility. "I knew there was no one who was going to take care of me if I got in trouble, and I had never lived a carefree lifestyle anyway. It was easy for me to understand that God's protection depended on my obedience, and I wanted to be faithful to him in everything I did."

Despite her new relationship with God, Kate began to feel increasingly burdened by her past. She was unable to relax, and she felt resentful of Christian friends who spent money freely or who failed to take life as seriously as she thought they should. Frequently, members of her prayer group advised her to "rest in the Lord," but fear of losing self-control prevented Kate from surrendering herself more fully to God. "When you grow up without responsible parents, there's no order in your life," Kate says. "I had to make my own order by being responsible, and I was deeply afraid of losing my hard-earned self-control. My memory of crying as a teenager was a wrenching shaking of my whole being, and I thought if I let my guard down, even for a minute, I would completely fall apart."

The turning point for Kate came after an automobile accident in which she received serious injury. While waiting for the ambulance, she felt prompted to pray for all those who had gathered to help her, including an exceptionally kind young man from a neighboring town. Several weeks later, while still recuperating, Kate received word that the young man had been in a boating accident and was drowned in a whirlpool because he was wearing hip-boots. "The Lord spoke to me about those boots," Kate recalls. "I saw myself as a small child walking through a swampy forest. I was wearing hip-boots for protection. Then suddenly I was in a boat, and God was telling me to take the boots off; I didn't need them anymore. My situation had changed, and the boots which had once protected me were now dangerous. If I kept them on and a storm arose, I would drown."

For Kate, it was a moment of insight into the past which enabled her to begin surrendering to God the hurts of her childhood. "When I was a child, my life really was a swamp," she says. "I needed to be self-sufficient and controlling. Even learning how to manipulate people was a matter of survival. My basic psychological and emotional needs weren't being met at home and I needed recognition from the outside world. But now God was asking me to give up the hip-boots which I still thought were indispensable. He showed me that my life was different now. I wasn't on my own, and I had outer and inner strengths which weren't available to me as a child. I came to understand that those hip-boots were from God, but they were only useful for a time. They didn't serve a purpose anymore. If I didn't get rid of them, they would drag me under when life became difficult."

For family members of an alcoholic, the surrender of old defense mechanisms, hurtful memories, anger, and resentment is an essential step to spiritual and mental health. Such surrender rarely takes place in a single moment; rather, it requires a long-term commitment to honesty and open communication. "These shadows from the past come to light only through times of confrontation and struggle," says Kate. "It is only with much prayer, through times of 'sitting with the Lord,' and by receiving good counsel from trusted and mature friends that I am learning not to react in the same old way. I have to consciously commit myself not to try to control others, not to manipulate them, even if I can justify it by thinking it's for their own good, or for the good of God's kingdom. It's hard to give up behavior which worked so well for so many years, and I'm still not totally free from it. But I'm learning day by day to rest in the Lord, and to release my life into his hands."

For family members who still live with an alcoholic, the process of surrender includes releasing the alcoholic to God's care and detaching themselves from his ups and downs. For most people, the key to this detachment is the acceptance of the disease model of addiction. Families who persist in viewing the alcoholic as a bad person in need of punishment, in my experience, inevitably get trapped in their own family sickness. It is only when they begin to see the alcoholic as a sick person in need of help that they find the spiritual and emotional resources they need for their own recovery.

STEP 4: Learn New Ways to Communicate

After years of living with an alcoholic, most family members have little understanding of the principles which govern good adult communication. They have spent too many years using words to attack or defend. Now they must learn, or relearn, the art of *speaking the truth in love*. While during the intervention process it was important for family members to control or mask their feelings, once the alcoholic is past the first shaky months of sobriety, the family must begin to communicate in a more honest fashion. At some point, family members should sit down with a third party, preferably a professional alcoholism counselor, and explain to the alcoholic how it was for them when he was drinking. Anger, sadness, hurt, shame, and guilt should be expressed in a direct, nonjudgmental manner so that the alcoholic can hear and digest what his family is saying. If family members resort to old methods of attack, the alcoholic's defense mechanisms will deafen him to the truth; but if they speak to him with loving concern, it is possible that he will understand, for the first time, the pain his addictive behavior has caused his family. With this understanding, the alcoholic and his family can confess their sins and give the forgiveness which leads to true restoration in relationships.

STEP 5: Find Outside Interests

Frequently the drinking alcoholic becomes the center of attention for his entire family, and for some members his behavior and moods become a full-blown obsession. Whether or not the alcoholic recovers, it is important that family members learn to remove him from the center of their thoughts and that they fill the resulting vacuum with new interests and activities. For some, stepping out of the alcoholic's orbit takes an enormous amount of courage, and initially they will need a great deal of support from friends and other family members. The reward for this difficult step is as great as the diversity and beauty of God's world, and as family members expand the boundaries of their experience with new hobbies, service to others, cultivation of their personal gifts, and church involvement, they will discover for themselves an old and important truth: Idolatry takes many forms, and only God himself is worthy of being at the center of our thoughts and energies.

When family members follow their own steps to recovery and commit themselves to supporting the alcoholic in his program of recovery, the prospects for their future are very bright. At the same time, anyone involved with a recovering alcoholic needs to know that many individuals have one or more relapses before becoming permanently sober. For this reason, it is important that the alcoholic and his family understand the symptoms of relapse and that they learn how to respond appropriately if the alcoholic should begin drinking again.

22

Relapse

Evelyn was an active member of Alcoholics Anonymous for over seven years. She attended AA meetings on a daily basis, was a frequent speaker at national and international conferences on addiction, and became an influential member of a government task force on alcoholism. Her work brought her into daily contact with the rich and the powerful, and she was able to help many men and women from the upper levels of society find help for their drinking problems.

As Evelyn's influence expanded, she became increasingly opinionated and aware of her own importance. At work, she was dictatorial; among friends, she was irritable and unpredictable. She angrily abused co-workers who disagreed with her and broke off relationships at the slightest provocation. As her speaking schedule became more demanding, she had less and less time for old friends and, unless invited to speak, she seldom attended AA meetings.

One night, while traveling home by plane from a national conference on alcoholism, Evelyn ordered a cocktail. It was only an experiment. For years she had heard other recovering alcoholics say, "It's the first drink that gets you drunk," but now she was certain she had been sober long enough to handle one drink. Evelyn was right—one drink was all she wanted. She was elated to discover how easily she controlled her drinking. From now on, as long as she wasn't with friends from AA, she intended to enjoy an occasional drink.

For over a year Evelyn drank socially and slowly fell back into addictive drinking. One drink became two, two became three, until suddenly she was rushing home from work every evening to pour herself a glass of wine. Her behavior deteriorated rapidly, and she began to hate herself for the angry, rude person she had become. She plunged into deep depression and, too ashamed to ask for help, she began to plan her own death.

Urged on by the intervention of an insightful friend and despite her own embarrassment, Evelyn entered the treatment center where she had directed dozens of other alcoholics. Before long she was hearing voices urging her to kill herself, and eventually she suffered a complete nervous breakdown. During this time, her confusion and fear compelled her to admit her powerlessness over her life, and she threw herself on the mercy of the God she wasn't even sure she believed in. Her self-surrender on the balcony of the treatment center led to a dramatic conversion, and she gave herself and her fears to Jesus Christ.

Today, the only thing that surprises Evelyn is that she waited seven years to start drinking again. "All those years I was in AA, I was an agnostic," she says. "I ignored the spiritual principles, and although I highly recommended the twelve steps to others, I never practiced them myself. I thought I was doing great without them. Instead, I was setting myself up for a relapse.

"Today, I am convinced that these twelve steps are God's invitation to sanctity for people who suffer from addiction. I'm not saying they have made me perfect. I still stumble and fall, I'm still often defiant and full of myself or intolerant of others. But day by day I can see important changes. And I face each day with faith and hope, confident that in the end it will all work out as a loving and merciful God wills."

Like Evelyn, the vast majority of recovering alcoholics who begin to drink again do so not because they are caught off guard by a sudden craving, but because they allow themselves to slide into careless thinking and living.

This carelessness leads to cockiness and overconfidence. As the recovering alcoholic loses his respect for the power of alcohol, he easily convinces himself that one or two drinks won't hurt. When he finally drinks again, it is seldom with the intention of getting drunk; rather, his goal is to prove that he can now drink like other people. Unfortunately, for most recovering alcoholics, one drink leads to a drunk or, as in the case of Evelyn, a drink or two without repercussions feeds the illusion of control, and the recovering alcoholic slowly slides back into compulsive drinking.

Perhaps the most startling aspect of relapse is the ease with which the physical, psychological, and spiritual consequences of addiction reassert themselves. The biological adjustments which the body once made to adapt itself to the constant presence of alcohol can be recreated almost instantly, even after years of abstinence, and withdrawal symptoms may reappear in less than a day. Crippling feelings of anxiety, guilt, and self-hatred return with intensified power, and the recovering alcoholic quickly reverts to rationalizing and denying his drinking problem. He falls into old patterns of behaving with family members, and in many cases his addiction progresses even more rapidly than it did during his former drinking days.

Maria was an alcoholism counselor who had been sober for twenty years when she met and married a prosperous building contractor. One night shortly after their marriage, Maria's husband took her out to dinner and urged her to try a drink. Eager to please, Maria ordered a gin and tonic. Two weeks later, she was in the critical care unit of our hospital, nearly dead from alcoholic hepatitis. She was in a substantially more advanced stage of alcoholism than when she quit drinking twenty years earlier, and she never completely recovered from the acute physical damage caused by her relapse.

"I know that I have another drunk left in me," say many recovering alcoholics. "I just don't know if I have another recovery." Although relapse is not necessarily fatal, it is also not inevitable. Certainly, it is far easier to prevent its occurrence than it is to pick up the pieces

after the recovering alcoholic is drinking again. Most recovering alcoholics signal their approaching relapse by
adopting dry-drunk behavior; they become impatient,
easily bored, resentful, judgmental, and full of grandiose
ideas. They overreact to minor difficulties, and their actions become as rigid and thoughtless as they were during
their drinking days. They often become either unusually
depressed or euphoric, and they begin once again to
blame others for their own shortcomings.

In an effort to avoid relapse, many recovering alcoholics find it helpful to take a periodic inventory of their
behavior with the aid of a wife or husband, a close friend,
or a spiritual advisor. The list of symptoms which appears
on pages 173–175 summarizes the potential trouble spots,
and recovering alcoholics as well as their family members
and friends should familiarize themselves with these
warning signs. Recovering alcoholics need not live in fear
of relapse—a person who is afraid of drinking may drink
to overcome that fear—but it is essential that they maintain an accurate perspective on the power of alcohol and
their own potential weaknesses.

What if the Recovering Alcoholic Drinks Again?

Because of the speed at which addiction progresses after relapse, it is important that family members and
friends act immediately if they discover that the recovering alcoholic has returned to drinking. Some recovering
alcoholics will ask for help; otherwise, a second intervention should be arranged, following the guidelines found in
Chapter 15. The recovering alcoholic should be encouraged to attend again either a treatment center or ninety
meetings of Alcoholics Anonymous in ninety days. In my
opinion, any recovering alcoholic who has one or more
relapses should commit himself to lifelong participation in
AA.

It is important that family members not panic during
relapse and that they avoid falling back into old patterns
of reacting to the alcoholic. Every chronic illness tends

A Checklist of Symptoms Leading to Relapse*

1. **Exhaustion.** Allowing yourself to become overly tired or in poor health. Some alcoholics are also prone to work addictions—perhaps they are in a hurry to make up for lost time. Good health and enough rest are important. If you feel good, you are more apt to think well. Feel poor and your thinking is apt to deteriorate. Feel bad enough and you might begin thinking a drink couldn't make it any worse.
2. **Dishonesty.** This begins with a pattern of unnecessary little lies and deceits with fellow workers, friends, and family. Then come important lies to yourself. This is called rationalizing—making excuses for not doing what you do not want to do, or for doing what you should not do.
3. **Impatience.** Things are not happening fast enough. Or others are not doing what they should or what you want them to.
4. **Argumentativeness.** Arguing small and ridiculous points of view indicates a need to always be right. "Why don't you be reasonable and agree with me?" Looking for an excuse to drink?
5. **Depression.** Unreasonable and unaccountable despair may occur in cycles and should be dealt with—talked about.
6. **Frustration.** At people and also because things may not be going your way. Remember—everything is not going to be just the way you want it.
7. **Self-Pity.** "Why do these things happen to me?" "Why must I be alcoholic?" Nobody appreciates all I am doing—(for them?)

---

*From *A Look at Relapse* by Charles W. Crewe copyright © 1974, by Hazelden Foundation, Center City, MN. Reprinted by permission.

8. **Cockiness.** Got it made—no longer fear alcoholism—going into drinking situations to prove to others you have no problem. Do this often enough and it will wear down your defenses.
9. **Complacency.** "Drinking was the farthest thing from my mind." Not drinking was no longer a conscious thought either. It is dangerous to let up on disciplines because everything is going well. Always to have a little fear is a good thing. More relapses occur when things are going well than otherwise.
10. **Expecting too much from others.** "I've changed; why hasn't everyone else?" It's a plus if they do—but it is still your problem if they do not. They may not trust you yet, may still be looking for further proof. You cannot expect others to change their life-styles just because you have.
11. **Letting up on disciplines.** Prayer, meditation, daily inventory, *A.A. Attendance.* This can stem either from complacency or boredom. You cannot afford to be bored with your program. The cost of relapse is always too great.
12. **Use of mood-altering chemicals.** You may feel the need to ease things with a pill, and your doctor may go along with you. You may never have had a problem with chemicals other than alcohol, but you can easily lose sobriety starting this way—about the most subtle way to have a relapse. Remember you will be cheating! The reverse of this is true for drug-dependent persons who start to drink.
13. **Wanting too much.** Do not set goals you cannot reach with normal effort. Do not expect too much. It's always great when good things you were not expecting happen. You will get what you are entitled to as long as you do your best, but maybe not as soon as you think you should. "Happiness is not having what you want, but wanting what you have."

---

14. **Forgetting gratitude.** You may be looking nega-
    tively on your life, concentrating on problems
    that still are not totally corrected. Nobody wants
    to be a Pollyanna—but it is good to remember
    where you started from—and how much better
    life is now.
15. **"It can't happen to me."** This is dangerous think-
    ing. Almost anything can happen to you and is
    more likely to if you get careless. Remember you
    have a progressive disease, and you will be in
    worse shape if you relapse.
16. **Omnipotence.** This is a feeling that results from a
    combination of many of the above. You now
    have all the answers for yourself and others. No
    one can tell you anything. You ignore sugges-
    tions or advice from others. Relapse is probably
    imminent unless drastic change takes place.

---

toward relapse, and while alcoholic relapse is dangerous
and should be avoided at all costs, it can be beneficial if
handled properly. The alcoholic should not be berated or
made to perceive himself as a failure; rather, he should be
encouraged to become aware of the behavior and attitudes which led to his relapse and to make adjustments in
his lifestyle that reduce further problems.

Some alcoholics have repeated relapses before they sober up permanently, and family members and friends
should not give up on a drinker just because he is having
difficulty maintaining his sobriety. One of my good
friends was in and out of Alcoholics Anonymous seven
times in six years before he was finally able to quit drinking. Many others have two or three relapses before they
permanently give up alcohol. In such cases, it is important to focus on the success of periods of sobriety, rather
than the acute pain of relapse. One alcoholism counselor
remarks:

I had a young patient who was addicted to alcohol, heroin, and tranquilizers. When I first met Jane she was getting high every day. After treatment, she was clean for eight months. She slipped, came back, and was drug-free for another fourteen months. Then she went on a drinking binge. Now it's been over two years that she's been without a drink or any other drug. A few months ago, she experienced a crushing disappointment when she learned that she no longer had the mental aptitude to fulfill her lifelong ambition to be a journalist. She weathered this crisis without resorting to drugs. Although in terms of recovery statistics, Jane's repeated relapses make her a failure, in my own eyes and in her own, she is a remarkable success.

One final word of warning must be given about relapse. There are at least one million recovering alcoholics in our world, and most of them choose to remain anonymous in keeping with the principles of AA. They are our friends, our fellow church members, and our co-workers, and what they need from us is support, not temptation. For example, Angela is a recovering alcoholic and a nurse, working in a hospice for terminally ill patients. One night after a particularly bad week, her hospital chaplain encouraged the entire hospice staff to unwind with a bottle of champagne. Angela, not wanting to reject his gift, took one drink, and then four more. For two weeks, she was engaged in a minute-by-minute battle with her craving for alcohol, and it was only through much prayer and counseling that she resisted temptation.

There are an extraordinary number of people who try to pressure their friends or acquaintances into a drink, and all of us must be careful to refrain from leading a recovering alcoholic into difficulty. We must honor their struggle with alcohol by supporting their sobriety and by being careful never to entice anyone to drink.

What if the Alcoholic Never Stops Drinking?

Billie Jean realized that her husband was an alcoholic the night her third child was born. "I asked Don to take care of our two small children while I was in the hospital," she remembers. "He loved them very much, but he got drunk anyway, and I knew he was no longer in control of his drinking."

For the next twenty years, Billie Jean adjusted her life to make room for an alcoholic husband. She stopped inviting friends home, became both father and mother to her children, and accepted without complaining her husband's unchanging daily routine of working, drinking, and sleeping. Don was never physically violent, but no one in the family was spared from his cruel verbal abuse. "Living in an environment of unrelenting criticism and constant accusation is like the slow dripping of water on a rock," says Billie Jean. "Eventually, even strong people get worn down. But I wasn't a strong person. I grew up wanting to please everyone, and I idolized my husband. I wanted him to love me, and I gradually let him take more and more control of my life. When I saw how much he was hurting the children, I thought of leaving him, but I was too emotionally and financially dependent to be on my own. I didn't think I could support myself and the kids, and even though Don was drunk most of the time, I couldn't imagine life without him."

Shortly after her last child left home, Billie Jean began to seek a deeper relationship with God and, with the help of Christian friends, she found a new sense of security and self-worth. Don was disturbed by the changes in Billie Jean's behavior, and he stepped up his efforts to control their relationship. "He decided to move to a new town," Billie Jean remembers. "I didn't have the courage to say no, so I went with him. Away from old friends and our family, Don was the only person in my life. My old feelings of dependency returned, but there wasn't anything to depend on. I was exhausted by the effort of living with Don's unpredictable anger and constant negativity. Finally I went to bed one day and told God I wasn't getting up until he spoke to me. All day long, the thought kept coming to me, 'Make it impossible for me to stay.' If I had it to do over again, I would have left right then.

"It seemed from that moment on, God's grace for living with my husband was removed. There was a strong sense of evil in our house, and I was always afraid of what Don might do next. During this time, Don went to a doctor for liver problems, but he refused to make any effort to get help for his drinking. I lost hope that he would ever get better."

Within a year, Billie Jean packed up her clothes and left her husband. She was fifty-two years old; she had no college diploma or prior work experience, and she was without any means of financial support. "It was the Lord who gave me confidence to make a move," Billie Jean recalls. "He provided for the details of my life—a place to live, a job, good friends—and I was always conscious of his presence and sustaining love."

Today, Billie Jean has completed college and graduate school, and she is teaching in a community college. Her husband is still drinking, and in eight years she has never returned to her former home. "A few months ago a woman asked me if my failure in marriage affected my ability to serve God," says Billie Jean. "But I don't see myself as a failure. It is naïve to think that everyone will respond to my love—not everyone responded even to the perfect love of Jesus—and although I still love Don, I'm not going to live with him while he is drinking. Sometimes people encourage me to go back to him, but I think they would be less eager to see me return if they knew what a miracle it was that I was finally able to leave."

It is a sad and unavoidable truth that many alcoholics persistently refuse help and give no sign of ever recovering from their addiction. In these cirumstances, family members and even close friends must make hard personal decisions about their future relationship with the alcoholic. Although there are no simple rules that apply to every situation, it is helpful to consider the following points when making such decisions.

1. *Under no circumstances should family members continue to live with a physically violent alcoholic.* There are community resources for the protection of battered spouses and their children. Family members who experi-

ence physical battering should remove themselves from the alcoholic's presence as soon as possible.

2. *Verbal abuse and unpredictable cruel behavior can be even more damaging than physical violence.* When the alcoholic becomes a psychological and spiritual threat to his family, it is time for a separation. This separation should not end until the alcoholic quits drinking. With the help of church leaders and other professional helpers, husbands and wives must make their own individual decisions concerning legal actions and divorce.

3. *Money is a great weapon.* People who are financially dependent upon a drinking alcoholic should begin to prepare themselves to be self-supporting, even if they do not plan to leave the alcoholic. One of my patients stayed with her drinking husband long enough to get a business degree and find full-time employment, and then left to protect herself and her children from further physical and emotional damage.

4. *Family members and friends must be patient with wives or husbands who regularly leave their husbands or wives only to return within a few weeks or months to an unchanged situation.* Particularly in cases of physical and/or emotional abuse, many wives and husbands must leave and return several times before they are able to make a final decision. Such people need continuous support from their friends. Even though their indecision and unpredictability tax the patience of all those involved, it is important to understand that for many people repeated coming and going is a natural part of the separation process.

5. *Husbands and wives who have left alcoholic marriages should not be counseled to return to them while the alcoholic is still drinking.* Only a very few people in special circumstances are able to live with a drinking alcoholic and not be destroyed by him or her. A "marriage at all cost" attitude is unrealistic and dangerous.

6. *The church must take seriously its pastoral role for people whose marriages and families fall apart because of*

addiction. These people need the same sympathy and compassion that is given to families during times of death, and they should be encouraged to give themselves time for mourning. It is important to remember that because family members of alcoholics almost always internalize the alcoholic's accusations, they are normally burdened by crippling feelings of guilt. They need strong reassurance that they are not responsible for the alcoholic's continued drinking, and must be reminded that no one can cause or cure another's addiction. Words of consolation should be reinforced with a message of hope and mercy: The alcoholic may yet stop drinking, and family members can look ahead to their own future with excitement and gratitude for God's continued work of redemption in their lives.

23

A Call to Action

When I was a kid, I was jealous of my friends and their families. Our house was just a place to eat and sleep; we didn't talk to each other. At meals, everyone was quiet—unless there was an all-out war. It got so I was only happy when I was drunk, and I became an alcoholic before I was thirteen. When my parents found out, they made me go to a treatment center, and they went to Al-Anon. That's how they figured out that they were alcoholics too. So they started going to AA meetings. Today, things are different in our family. We sit down for meals together. We joke around and talk things over. It's the little things we do as a family—like going out and stuff. Mostly now I take it for granted, but sometimes when I think about it I start to cry.

Daniel, age 16

While my daughter was addicted, I let things drift. I became spiritually barren, and I felt guilty and afraid all the time. Even after she began her recovery, I had panic spells. At night I was attacked by ominous, free-floating anxiety; it seemed as if at any moment something I hadn't counted on could come from out of nowhere to grab my child and drag her under. But I've learned to let go and to trust God. Sometimes I can't believe all the things I've been able to surrender to his care. I don't try to carry the burdens of the world anymore. I've given up trying to fix things for my daughter, and I've stopped always trying to make peace between family

members. I've learned to let them work out their own problems. And through it all my daughter is like a flower that has
opened up. She was closed up tight for so many years, we
forgot what a wonderful human being was trapped inside.
Now, she can give love, and receive it, and she has blossomed
into a beautiful young lady.

>   Delores,
>   mother of a young adult alcoholic

From the beginning, God has been in the business of taking
what seems like tragedy and turning it into a blessing. He did
it in my life, and I have everything in the world to be grateful
for. After drinking to oblivion almost every night for fifteen
years, I sobered up with the help of AA. Then another recovering alcoholic led me to Jesus. There is so much joy in
knowing him. Of course, the physical consequences of my
addiction are still there. I've lost part of my stomach, my
memory isn't what it was, and I don't have the energy I once
did. All this once depressed me, but it doesn't concern me
anymore. I should have been dead twenty years ago; God has
restored to me so much more than I ever lost, and I know
that every day I'm alive is a gift from him.

A few months ago, our nineteen-year-old son was killed in
an automobile accident. I think it's true what they say: No
one knows the pain of losing a child until it happens to them.
But the miracle for me was that I could go through my son's
death and the devastation I still feel without ever thinking of
taking a drink. I used to get drunk if I had a flat tire. But God
has made me a new person. In Alcoholics Anonymous, we
call it "a spiritual awakening," a personality change at the
deepest levels of life. So I'm grateful I can be sober today. I
am able to be a comfort and strength to my wife and children; we are all going through this time of grief together; and
amazingly I have no doubts about eternal life or salvation.
Although it's still hard to know my son is gone, I am sure
beyond any question that he is with the Lord today, and I
know that we will be together again.

>   Cort, age 58

Restoration and redemption. The good news for each
one of us, whatever our life struggles may be, is that God

is able to save our lives from destruction. When choices made from ignorance or in rebellion to divine principles lead us into captivity, when we waste our gifts and talents in pursuit of harmful or meaningless goals, the final word has yet to be spoken about our lives. God can restore "the years the locusts have eaten" (Joel 2:25). He can turn our most grievous defeats into victory and our crippling weaknesses into an opportunity to experience his strength and mercy. Step by step, day by day, through repentance and in quiet service to the Lord, our broken lives can be transformed into glorious reflections of our Creator.

This transforming power of God's grace is nowhere more desperately needed in our society than in the areas of alcohol abuse and addiction. In a recent Gallup Poll, a staggering one out of three persons reported that alcohol had caused trouble in their families. Heavy drinking is involved in 60 percent of violent crimes, 30 percent of all suicides, 80 percent of fire and drowning accidents. Every twenty-two minutes another life is lost to a drunk driver. The cost to our society is conservatively estimated at fifty billion per year in the United States alone, and beyond these staggering statistics lie the ruined and priceless lives of millions of men, women, and children.

The overwhelming need of society, the pronounced spiritual dimension of addiction, and the hope of restoration and redemption are compelling reasons for Christian believers to involve themselves in the issues of alcohol abuse and addiction. Like David, the Jewish king, those of us who follow Jesus Christ must learn to "serve our generation" at its point of need with practical and effective efforts. Toward this end, it is important that we give serious consideration to (1) examining our own drinking habits, (2) equipping our churches for action, and (3) participating in community prevention efforts.

Alcoholism and the Church.

When Andrew admitted himself to an alcoholism treatment center, his wife turned to the church they recently joined for help. "It was incredible," his wife remembers.

"We were overwhelmed by an outpouring of love and support. Andrew received so many cards and letters in treatment that his fellow patients thought he was a celebrity. Dozens of people prayed for him every day, and the elders set aside time for a special prayer service. They laid hands on me and prayed for both of us. It was an experience with the Lord that I will never forget. Then, when Andrew finally returned home from treatment, our pastor publicly welcomed him back, and the whole church broke out into applause. Andrew and I will always be indebted to these friends who played such an important role in his recovery."

With a small investment of time and effort, any church can equip itself to minister to alcoholics and their families. The rewards for this ministry are enormous. Recovering alcoholics are among the most spiritually vibrant Christians I know, and the enthusiasm and commitment they bring to their relationship with Christ contribute greatly to the spiritual health of the churches they attend. For any church interested in establishing a ministry for alcoholics, important first steps include:

1. *Identify Resource People.* Every church should have a core of people who have educated themselves about alcohol and other drug addictions. Where possible, this group should include recovering alcoholics and persons with past involvement in other forms of drug dependency. Not every church needs to have its own counseling service, but anyone who does counseling of any kind should be able to recognize the early symptoms of alcohol and drug addiction. They should also know where to take alcoholics and drug addicts for detoxification. Church doors should be opened to groups such as Alcoholics Anonymous and Al-Anon so that they can hold their meetings. In addition, members of the core group should familiarize themselves with local treatment facilities.

2. *Educate the Congregation and the Community.* When the core group is adequately educated, they in turn

can teach their fellow church members and the outside community through films, workshops, Bible studies, and lectures.

It is important that ministers also support this effort from the pulpit. With sermons and short talks they can help their congregation become aware of the danger of addiction and give them guidelines for developing a biblical view of the use of alcohol and drugs. A recent poll of my denomination showed that 83 percent of the ministers believed that the church should do something about alcohol abuse, but over 70 percent never had preached a sermon on the subject![1] I suspect this silence originates at least in part from a desire to avoid identification with strident antidrinking groups who make smoking and drinking a test of fellowship among Christian believers. Whatever the motivation, the time for silence is past. Ministers must work to find creative and persuasive ways to talk to their congregations about the problem of alcohol abuse and addiction.

A word of warning about efforts to alert young people to the dangers of alcohol. Scare tactics are notoriously ineffective. Rigid attitudes and dogmatic approaches undermine credibility and usually result in teenagers dismissing the information they receive. This natural rebellion against manipulation is one of the reasons children of dogmatic teetotalers are at unusually high risk for developing alcohol addiction. In any case, Mark Twain's advice is well-taken: "Temperate temperance is best. Intemperate temperance injures the cause of temperance." The best way to educate children and adults about alcohol is to give them information in an objective and non-alarmist fashion, and allow proper behavior to grow out of their desire to do what is right or their instinct for self-preservation.

3. *Encourage Attitudes of Compassion.* Betty Wilson (Chapter 2) belongs to a small church group which meets every week for two hours of Bible study and intercessory prayer. Despite the intimate communication which frequently takes place in the group, Betty refuses to tell any-

one that she is a recovering alcoholic. "I've heard them talk about alcoholics," Betty says. "I know what they would think of me if I said I had the same problem. For the sake of our friendships, I keep this part of my life a secret." The truth is that Betty is only one of two recovering alcoholics in her small group; another woman also feels compelled to keep silent about her addiction because she fears her friends' reaction.

Sadly, such fears are well-founded. Studies show that people with strong religious convictions have harsher attitudes toward alcoholics than those for whom religion is completely unimportant.[2] And it is well known among groups of recovering alcoholics that churches are generally unaccepting of their addiction. Many recovering alcoholics with whom I am acquainted refuse to attend church because of their memory of the condemning attitude of Christian believers.

"Everyone in this world is some kind of weakling," said the late Reverend Sam Shoemaker, addressing a group of recovering alcoholics. "If he thinks he is not, then pride is his weakness, and it is the greatest weakness of all." The basis of Christian fellowship, Shoemaker added, is found not in our human goodness, but in our common need for forgiveness and healing. "The church has always been a scratch company of sinners. It is not the best people in the community, gathered together for self-congratulation; it is the people who know they have a great need, gathered to find its answer in worship toward God and fellowship with one another. The church is not a museum; it is a hospital."[3]

When Christian believers have a proper perception of themselves and the role of the church, they are free to share the spiritual resources of their congregation with alcoholics, whether they are recovering or still drinking. Chief among these resources are prayer and healing services, the laying on of hands, the fellowship of small prayer groups, and participation in communion and worship. The church also has an opportunity to be a family to people who have no families, or who come from broken families, and ministries of hospitality and healing should extend not only to alcoholics but to their wives and husbands, parents and children, and even close friends.

One of the special missions of the church is to minister to Christian believers who become alcoholics. The guilt and shame felt by Christian alcoholics is even more pronounced than that of their secular counterparts. Often, long after they stop drinking, they live in fear that God has permanently rejected them. Such individuals often need extensive counseling before they are able to believe that their sins have been forgiven and that God still has a personal and loving concern for their lives.

Personal Drinking Habits:
The Need for Self-Examination

The Christian community, throughout history, has taken a number of different views toward alcoholic beverages. The Bible indicates that Jews and early Christian believers drank fermented beverages. In the more recent history of the United States, the Puritans were inclined to agree with the Israelites that wine was a gift from God "that gladdens the heart of man." (Psalm 104:15). However, as alcohol abuse and alcoholism became enormous social problems in the nineteenth and early twentieth centuries, church leaders and other social reformers began to advocate total abstinence as the only socially responsible attitude towards alcohol. Liberals and conservatives alike hailed the passage of the Prohibition Amendment in 1919. In his funeral address for "John Barleycorn," the revivalist Billy Sunday spoke for many: "Good-bye John. The reign of tears is over. The slums will soon be only a memory. We will turn our prisons into factories and our jails into storehouses and corncribs. Men will walk upright now, women will smile, and the children will laugh. Hell will be forever for rent."[4]

Despite its success in lowering the incidence of alcoholism and alcohol-related problems, prohibition proved unworkable. Today, alcohol plays a significant role in American culture, and heavy drinking is not just accepted but encouraged. In this environment, more and more Christian believers have relaxed their opposition to social drinking and many have adopted drinking habits that resemble those of society as a whole.

As we examine our own drinking habits, it is important to remember that opinions about the use of alcohol should not be viewed as a test of faith and fellowship. While the Bible speaks clearly against drunkenness, there is no clear statement against drinking itself, and since the beginning of the church, Christians have been drinking as a matter of personal liberty. At the same time, I think there are good reasons why all of us should give total abstinence serious consideration.

First, anyone who has any evidence of addiction in their family history—grandparents, uncles, aunts, fathers, mothers, brothers, sisters—should avoid drinking alcohol. As we have seen, heredity unquestionably plays a role in addiction, and persons with a family history of alcoholism are at high risk for becoming alcoholics themselves. Recently, a man who descended from four generations of alcoholics asked me if that meant he would have to give up even an occasional beer with the boys. I had to tell him, "That's exactly what it means." In the presence of a family history, any drinking is foolish.

Second, despite the pronounced role of heredity, there is no way to predict who will or will not become an alcoholic. What we do know is that one out of ten social drinkers will become alcoholics, and that the majority of these will drift into addiction *unconsciously.* Given the odds, many people may understandably conclude that an ounce of prevention is worth a pound of cure and opt for total abstinence.

Third, I believe that ministers, elders, deacons, and other church leaders should consider the "Nazarite vow" as ideal and abstain from drinking altogether. While we ourselves may have no trouble with alcohol, there are people who pattern their behavior after our own, and we must be careful not to lead them into trouble. There is also the danger of intoxication; a church leader who drinks and occasionally gets tipsy lowers the spiritual power he has available for his people. Drunkenness, even

if it is accidental, quenches the Holy Spirit and it is un-
wise for a church leader to take that risk.

Finally, all Christians need to consider seriously the effect that alcohol has on the part of our brain that controls
inhibitions. As followers of Jesus, we are involved in spiritual warfare and constantly facing temptations. Even
when we are at our best, when our inhibitions are in full
force, it is often difficult to resist the subtle strategems of
Satan. To deliberately lower our inhibitions in a time of
warfare is a risk many of us will be unwilling to take.

Community Prevention Efforts

Working with alcoholics and their families is much like
standing at the base of a cliff, picking up the bodies of
victims who have fallen over the edge. A person can only
work there so long before he begins to think about climb-
ing to the top and building a fence to prevent people from
wandering too close to the edge.

Unfortunately, in contemporary society there are numerous forces which encourage heavy drinking regardless of the cost in lives and productivity. Worldwide, the
liquor industry spends some 2 billion dollars annually to
advertise alcoholic beverages. Their efforts are aimed at
new groups of drinkers like women, young people, and
the Third World. Advertising has been particularly effective in poor countries. Adding to their already staggering
economic and social problems, developing countries increased their imports of alcohol from 325 million to 1.3
billion dollars in a ten-year period.[5] In the United States,
where affluence and materialism create problems of their
own, sports and entertainment figures bombard television
viewers with the message that drinking is the ticket to
success, happiness, and the good life. "If you can manage
to get some of the powers of the liquor industry talking
off the record," says one prominent alcoholism re-
searcher, "they will tell you that they never sell alcohol;
they really sell sex and sophistication. The alcohol is
merely a subliminal partner. . . . Children pick up these
signals. That's education."[5]

This education is reinforced by the remarkable amount of free publicity received by the liquor industry through magazine stories, comic books, newspaper articles, and most importantly, television. A recent study of the top ten television shows revealed that, while smoking incidents have remarkably decreased, an average of more than eight alcoholic drinks are taken per television hour.[7] Authorities agree that this constant flow of alcohol results in the "normalization" of drinking. It becomes understood by our children and throughout our society that the consumption of alcoholic beverages is necessary to lead a satisfying life.

In the midst of this overwhelming support for society's number one mind-altering drug, there are many fence-building efforts to which individuals and churches can contribute time and money. These preventive measures include:

- removing advertisements for alcoholic beverages from television
- raising taxes on alcohol until it is priced out of the reach of most teenagers (consumption of alcohol even among adults is directly related to cost)
- placing warning labels on liquor bottles
- working against drunk driving and student drug use
- helping civic groups and schools disseminate information on addiction and its treatment

Individuals interested in participating in any of these activities can contact the organizations listed in Appendix C for further information.

In all these efforts perhaps our most effective action is to help one another and teach our children to cope with difficulty and to experience joy without resorting to chemical reinforcement. As our culture becomes increasingly devoted to the pursuit of pleasure and more and more accustomed to the instant relief of pain, we must reaffirm our commitment to live as God's children. In the joy and comfort of his Holy Spirit, we can give sober service to him, as we wait in faith for the final restoration of all creation.

I waited patiently for the Lord;
   he turned to me and heard my cry.
He lifted me out of the slimy pit,
   out of the mud and mire;
He set my feet on a rock
   and gave me a firm place to stand.
He put a new song in my mouth,
   a hymn of praise to our God.
Many will see and fear
   and put their trust in the Lord.

Psalm 40

Appendixes

APPENDIX A

VANDERBILT UNIVERSITY MEDICAL CENTER
NASHVILLE, TENNESSEE 37232

Primary Care Center • Division of General Internal Medicine

PERSONAL AND CONFIDENTIAL

John Doe
Vanderbilt University
Nashville, Tennessee

Dear John:

At the request of your grandfather, Jack Doe, I am writing you as his physician and a close personal friend. All of the grandchildren of college age in your family will be receiving this letter, and I would appreciate hearing your thoughts on this matter.

As you know, your grandfather is recovering from alcoholism. He is doing extremely well, and we are all grateful that he has received treatment and is maintaining an active role in Alcoholics Anonymous.

You may well be asking, "What does this have to do with me?" I want to alert you to the fact that heredity plays a strong role in the development of alcoholism. It is thought that the majority of our nation's 10 million alcoholics come from families with an inherited tendency, and recent medical research has supplied compelling evidence for this claim. In one patient sub-group study, sons of alcoholic fathers adopted at birth had a 9 to 1 chance of developing an addiction over children adopted at birth from nonalcoholic fathers. The transmission from mother to daughter stood at 3 to 1. These extraordinary statistics are supported by the personal experience of alcoholism counselors, and at any meeting of Alcoholics Anonymous, it is likely that between 60 to 80 percent of those present have relatives (fathers, mothers, brothers, sisters, aunts, uncles, grandparents) who are alcoholics.

The evidence in your own family is equally striking. Joseph Doe, born in 1861 and the brother of your great grandfather, was an alcoholic. Philip Doe, your uncle, is also an alcoholic. And of course your grandfather is now recovering from the same disorder.

Perhaps you are wondering what we mean by "alcoholic."

Here it is important to distinguish between alcohol *abuse* and alcohol *addiction*. The alcohol abuser frequently drinks to intoxication and may suffer painful consequences from his excessive consumption. However, he can still choose when he drinks, how much he drinks, and if he drinks. The alcohol addict on the other hand is no longer in control of his own will, and he can not predict when or how much he will drink. He continues to drink even after alcohol is causing him serious problems with family, health, jobs, and finances, and he begins to organize his entire life around his need for a drink. Some of the symptoms of alcohol addiction include guilt and shame about drinking, increased anxiety, marriage problems, blackouts (periods of time when the drinker functions normally but later does not remember what he did), increasing consumption, preoccupation with drinking, and extreme mood swings.

I am writing this letter to inform you that, like your brothers, sisters, and cousins, you may have an inherited tendency towards addiction. Drinking alcoholic beverages is likely to be hazardous to your health, and repeated heavy drinking may lead you unawares into alcoholism. I trust that you will take this warning seriously, and that you will make an appropriate decision regarding your own drinking habits. If you have any questions or would like further information, please feel free to write or call.

We love you very much and desire for you happy, productive lives. You come from a distinguished family, and I am certain that you will make a unique contribution with your life. Please consider this letter a part of your education, and I look forward to meeting you one day.

Sincerely,

Anderson Spickard, Jr., M.D.
Professor of Medicine
Medical Director, Vanderbilt
    Institute for Treatment
    of Alcoholism

A Simple Test: Are You an Alcoholic?

The following is the Michigan Alcoholism Screening Test (MAST). Scoring is simple. *Yes* or *no* answers receive between 0 and 5 points, depending on the significance of the question. The test and scoring key are on the following pages. Total scores should be evaluated as follows:

0– 5	Not diagnostic of addiction
5– 7	Possible addiction
7–15	Early addiction
15–25	Moderate addiction
25 and over	Severe addiction

These scores represent generalizations and their accuracy depends upon the reliability of the answers given. Spouses or close friends of the alcoholic can take the test for the alcoholic with a 90 percent accuracy rating.

MAST Scoring Key

ITEM
1.	Yes 0	No 2
2.	Yes 2	No 0
3.	Yes 1	No 0
4.	Yes 0	No 2
5.	Yes 1	No 0
6.	Yes 0	No 2
7.	Yes 0	No 2
8.	Yes 5	No 0
9.	Yes 1	No 0
10.	Yes 2	No 0
11.	Yes 2	No 0
12.	Yes 2	No 0
13.	Yes 2	No 0
14.	Yes 2	No 0
15.	Yes 2	No 0
16.	Yes 1	No 0
17.	Yes 2	No 0
18.	Yes 2	No 0
19.	Yes 5	No 0
20.	Yes 5	No 0
21.	Yes 2	No 0
22.	Yes 2	No 0
23.	Yes 2	No 0
24.	Yes 2	No 0

Michigan Alcoholism Screening Test

Circle one

1. Do you feel you are a normal drinker? (By normal we mean you drink less than or as much as most other people.)   Yes   No

2. Have you ever awakened the morning after some drinking the night before and found that you could not remember a part of the evening?   Yes   No

3. Does your wife, husband, a parent, or other near relative ever worry or complain about your drinking?   Yes   No

4. Can you stop drinking without a struggle after one or two drinks?   Yes   No

5. Do you ever feel guilty about your drinking?   Yes   No

6. Do friends or relatives think you are a normal drinker?   Yes   No

7. Are you able to stop drinking when you want to?   Yes   No

8. Have you ever attended a meeting of Alcoholics Anonymous?   Yes   No

9. Have you ever gotten into physical fights when drinking?   Yes   No

10. Has drinking ever created problems between you and your wife, husband, a parent, or other near relative?   Yes   No

11. Has your wife, husband, a parent, or other near relative ever gone to anyone for help about your drinking?   Yes   No

12. Have you ever lost friends, girl friends or boy friends, because of your drinking?   Yes   No

Circle one

13. Have you ever gotten into trouble at work be-
    cause of your drinking?   Yes No

14. Have you ever lost a job because of drinking? Yes No

15. Have you ever neglected your obligations, your
    family, or your work for two or more days in a
    row because you were drinking?   Yes No

16. Do you drink before noon fairly often?   Yes No

17. Have you ever been told you have liver trouble?
    Cirrhosis?   Yes No

18. After heavy drinking have you ever had delirium
    tremens (DTs) or severe shaking, or heard voices
    or seen things that weren't really there?   Yes No

19. Have you ever gone to anyone for help about
    your drinking?   Yes No

20. Have you ever been in a hospital because of
    drinking?   Yes No

21. Have you ever been a patient in a psychiatric
    hospital or on a psychiatric ward of a general
    hospital where drinking was part of the problem
    that resulted in hospitalization?   Yes No

22. Have you ever been seen at a psychiatric or men-
    tal health clinic or gone to any doctor, social
    worker, or clergyman for help with any emo-
    tional problem, where drinking was part of the
    problem?   Yes No

23. Have you ever been arrested for drunken driving
    under the influence of alcoholic beverages?   Yes No

24. Have you ever been arrested, even for a few
    hours, because of other drunken behavior?   Yes No

Books

Alcoholics Anonymous. 3d ed. New York: World Services, Inc., 1976.

Black, Claudia. *It Will Never Happen to Me.* Denver: M.A.C. Printing and Publications Division, 1982.

Drews, Toby Rice. *Getting Them Sober.* South Plainfield, NJ: Bridge Publishing, Inc., 1980.

Johnson, Vernon E. *I'll Quit Tomorrow.* New York: Harper and Row, 1980.

Kinney, Jean, and Gwen Leaton. *Loosening the Grip.* St. Louis: C.V. Mosby Company, 1983.

Maxwell, Ruth. *The Booze Battle.* New York: Praeger Publishers, 1976.

Vaillant, George E. *The Natural History of Alcoholism.* Cambridge, MA: Harvard University Press, 1983.

Films

"Soft Is the Heart of a Child" (16 mm)
Gerald T. Rogers Productions
5225 Old Orchard Road No. 6
Skokie, IL 60077

Depicts the varied reactions of children to an alcoholic father. A school counselor helps the children and their mother while giving informative instructions to the audience (and her colleagues).

"Our Brothers Keeper" (16 mm)
Gerald T. Rogers Productions
5225 Old Orchard Road No. 6
Skokie, IL 60077

Dramatic presentation of the tragedy of alcoholism in a physician practicing in a typical American community. The enabling behavior of the family and colleagues is well portrayed in this film.

"I'll Quit Tomorrow" (16 mm or videocassette)
The Johnson Institute
10700 Olson Memorial Highway
Minneapolis, MN 55441

"Classic" film depicting the progression of alcoholism and a successful intervention.

Other Resources

Al-Anon
A.F.G., Inc.
P.O. Box 182
Madison Square Station
New York, NY 10159–0182

Alcoholics Anonymous World Services, Inc.
Box 459 Grand Central Station
New York, NY 10163

The Comprehensive Care Corporation
660 Newport Center Drive
Newport Beach, CA 92660

Hazelden Educational Services
Box 176
Center City, MN 55012

The Johnson Institute
10700 Olson Memorial Highway
Minneapolis, MN 55441

Mothers Against Drunk Drivers
5330 Primrose, Suite 146
Fair Oaks, CA 95628
(916) 966-MADD

National Council on Alcoholism
733 Third Avenue
New York, NY 10017

The Vanderbilt Institute for Treatment of Alcoholism
Fourth Floor, Zerfoss Building
Vanderbilt University Medical Center
Nashville, TN 37232
(615) 322-6158

Notes

Chapter 1

1. Tom Alibrandi, *Young Alcoholics* (Minneapolis: CompCare Publications, 1978), 7.

Chapter 2

1. George E. Vaillant, *The Natural History of Alcoholism* (Cambridge, MA: Harvard University Press, 1983), 74.
2. Ibid., 65.
3. C.R. Cloninger, M. Bohman, and S. Sigvardsson, "Inheritance of Alcohol Abuse: Cross-fostering Analysis of Adopted Men," *Archives of General Psychiatry*, 38 (1981): 861–8.
4. Calvin Trillin, "U.S. Journal: Gallup, New Mexico," *The New Yorker*, 25 September 1971, 108.
5. Vaillant, *Natural History*, 58.

Chapter 3

1. Marty Mann, *New Primer on Alcoholism* (New York: Holt, Rinehart, and Winston, 1950), 27.

Chapter 5

1. As quoted in Andrew Sorenson, *Alcoholic Priests* (New York: The Seabury Press, 1976), 158.
2. J.P. van Wartburg, "Biochemische aspekte des alkoholismus," *Chimia*, 33 (1979): 79–83.

Chapter 6

1. Vernon E. Johnson, *I'll Quit Tomorrow* (San Francisco: Harper and Row, 1980), 39.

Chapter 8

1. Johnson, *I'll Quit*, 41.
2. Anthony M., "Al-Anon," *Journal of the American Medical Association*, vol. 238, no. 10, 5 September 1977, 1062.
3. Summary report of AAMCs medical student graduation questionnaire survey (Washington, D.C.: Association of American Medical Colleges, 1981).
4. Mark Bloom, "Impaired Physicians: Medicine Bites the Bullet," *Medical World News*, 24 July 1978, 41.
5. "Workside Anti-Alcoholism Saves Jobs, Money," *Journal of the American Medical Association*, vol. 249, no. 18, 13 May 1983, 2433.

Chapter 10

1. John Boit Morse, *Don't Tell Me I'm Not an Alcoholic*, a pamphlet (Center City, MN: Hazelden Foundation), 4.
2. Joseph Kellerman, *A Guide for the Family of the Alcoholic*, a pamphlet (Charlotte, NC: Charlotte Council on Alcoholism Groups), 7.

Chapter 11

1. *A Letter to Our Alcoholic Dad*, a pamphlet (Center City, MN: Hazelden Foundation, 1977).
2. Torey L. Hayden, *Murphy's Boy* (New York: G.P. Putnam, 1983), 241.

Chapter 12

1. These and other similar categories for the roles adopted by children of alcoholics are commonly recognized and referred to in connection with alcoholism and its treatment.

Chapter 14

1. *Alcoholics Anonymous* (New York: Alcoholics Anonymous World Services, Inc., 1976), p. xxvi.
2. *Living with an Alcoholic with the Help of Al-Anon* (New York: Al-Anon Family Group Headquarters, Inc., 1980), introduction.

Chapter 18

1. Vaillant, *Natural History*, 197.
2. *Alcoholics Anonymous*, 58.

Chapter 20

1. Roque Fajardo, *Helping Your Alcoholic before He or She Hits Bottom* (New York: Crown Publishers, Inc., 1976), 150.
2. *Alcoholics Anonymous,* 66.
3. Ibid., 64–68.

Chapter 23

1. Willmar Thorkelson, "Alcoholism," *A.D.* (January 1982): 12.
2. Ruth C. Engs, "Drinking Patterns and Attitudes Toward Alcoholism of Australian Human Service Students," *Journal of Studies on Alcohol,* vol. 43, no. 5 (1982): 528.
3. Samuel M. Shoemaker, "The Spiritual Angle," *The Grapevine* (October 1955): 17–18.
4. Mark Noll, "America's Battle Against the Bottle," *Christianity Today,* vol. 23, 17 January 1979, 21.
5. Morton Mintz, "Alcohol, Inc.: Bartender to the World," *The Washington Post,* 4 September 1983, C2.
6. Morris Chafetz, "Carrie Nation Had a Drinking Problem," *Johns Hopkins Magazine* (March 1976): 14.
7. As cited in Margaret A. Fuad, ed., *Alcohol Network News* (February 1983): 4.

Index

About the Authors

ANDERSON SPICKARD, M.D., is Professor of Medicine and Director of the Division of General Internal Medicine at Vanderbilt Medical Center. He is also Medical Director of the Vanderbilt Institute for Treatment of Alcoholism. He has written and spoken extensively on the treatment of alcoholism. And in 1980 he was given special recognition for Outstanding Leadership and Contribution in the Field of Alcohol and Drug Abuse. He resides in Nashville, Tennessee, where he is an elder at the First Presbyterian Church.

BARBARA R. THOMPSON is a freelance writer. Since receiving her M.A. in Philosophy from the University of Notre Dame, she has written a book, *A Distant Grief,* as well as numerous interviews for *Christianity Today.* Currently she makes her home in Brevard, North Carolina.